reader development in practice

bringing literature to readers

reader development in practice

bringing literature to readers

edited by **Susan Hornby** and **Bob Glass**

facet publishing

Published by Facet Publishing,
7 Ridgmount Street, London WC1E 7AE
www.facetpublishing.co.uk

Facet Publishing is wholly owned by
CILIP: the Chartered Institute of Library
and Information Professionals.

*British Library Cataloguing in Publication
Data*
A catalogue record for this book is
available from the British Library.

ISBN 978-1-85604-624-4

First published 2008

Typeset from editors' disks in 11/14pt
University Old Style and Zurich Expanded
by Facet Publishing.
Printed and made in Great Britain by MPG
Books Ltd, Bodmin, Cornwall.

Contents

Contributors

Ann Barlow

Ann Barlow is Director of Courses for the Public at the University of Manchester. Having originally trained and qualified as a teacher, she subsequently studied information management and for some time lectured in that field at Manchester Metropolitan University. In her current post she combines her experience as a teacher with her skills in information management, in the organization of course delivery to adult learners. Ann has a particular interest in the use of information technology for delivering lifelong learning opportunities, both in a face-to-face context and at a distance. In managing the delivery of a distance learning course in Egyptology to students around the globe, who have varying access to libraries and bookshops, she has investigated the availability and accessibility of e-texts as a means of supporting learning.

Ann Cleeves

After dropping out of university, Ann took a number of temporary jobs before going back to college and training to be a probation officer.

After her marriage to ornithologist Tim, she spent four years on the tidal island of Hilbre. This was when she started writing.

For the National Year of Reading, Ann was made reader-in-residence for three library authorities. She went on to set up reading groups in prisons as part of the Inside Books project, became Cheltenham Literature Festival's first reader-in-residence and worked as associate trainer with the reader development organization Opening the Book. She is reader-in-residence for the Harrogate Crime-Writing Festival.

Ann's short film for Border TV, *Catching Birds*, won a Royal Television Society Award. In 2006 she won the Duncan Lawrie Dagger award for best crime novel of the year for *Raven Black*, the first volume of her *Shetland Quartet*. The second, *White Nights*, is published in 2008.

Linda Corrigan

Linda Corrigan has a first degree in English Studies from the University of Nottingham (1970), a postgraduate diploma in Librarianship from Liverpool Polytechnic (now John Moores University; 1971), a master's degree in Anglo-Saxon Studies from the University of Manchester (1993), a postgraduate diploma in Careers Education and Guidance (1997) from Nottingham Trent University and a PhD in Place-Name Studies (2006) from Manchester University.

She is a professional librarian and has worked in library and information services for over 30 years. Currently she works as a freelance consultant, trainer and lecturer. Her work experience covers workplace libraries, school libraries, local authority information services and six years as Reader Development Manager at the National Library for the Blind. Linda has extensive management and planning experience, and specializes in education and training for young people and adults, particularly in the field of inclusive library services for disabled people.

Dr Jane Davis

Dr Jane Davis started Get Into Reading (GIR) with a £500 grant in 2001. At the time of writing the project involves seven project workers, seven library staff members and approximately 25 volunteers, as well as hundreds of beneficiaries. GIR groups meet once a week for one to two hours. All the reading is shared, read aloud, usually by a trained facilitator but increasingly by members of the reading groups. GIR has just been commissioned to deliver reading group services involving service users, carers and staff across the Mersey Care Trust, an NHS mental health service provider.

Mike Garry

Mike Garry is a poet, librarian and publisher. His poetry focuses upon the beautiful ugliness of the city and its people.

His first book, *Men's Morning*, tells the tale of an inner-city sauna. His second book, *Mancunian Meander*, is a poetic journey around a city, its suburbs and people. His work has been read on BBC Radio Manchester, Radio 4, Granada, Channel M and MTV Base.

He has worked in residencies in Strangeways and Hindley prisons, and at the *Big Issue*, Manchester children's homes, Trafford Mental Health and the Poetry Society.

A stunning performer and winner of numerous slams (live poetry contests), he has performed throughout Europe, in Hong Kong and at the famous Nuyorican Poets café in New York.

A runner-up in the Poem for Manchester competition and 2007 UK Slam Championships he has been commissioned to write poems for Manchester United, UNICEF and numerous local authorities, and is one of the National Literacy Trust's Reading Champions.

Andrew Glass

Andrew Glass is a young musician and researcher who is a graduate of University College Chichester (2004). He has been a member of a number of writing groups and literary cabaret clubs, including Tongues & Strings (Chichester) and Magnetic North (Greenwich). He has recently had his work published in *Mouth Ogres*, a creative writing anthology.

Andrew is a performance artist who combines music and the written word to produce an eclectic mix of humorous and serious work. His repertoire is diverse and includes a range of standards from 'Grand Waltz' to 'Fly Me To The Moon', as well as his own works.

As a freelance writer for Academic Knowledge Ltd, he is regularly required to research, write and re-write to tight deadlines. It is in his capacity of researcher that he has contributed to Chapter 10 of this book, 'Beyond the Caxton Legacy'.

Bob Glass

Bob Glass is Undergraduate Programme Leader for the Department of Information and Communications at Manchester Metropolitan University. He is a Fellow of the Higher Education Academy, and also a qualified librarian with many years of experience in libraries, bookselling, publishing and higher education. His current areas of teaching and research are library resource management, library systems, network technologies, information literacy, Web 2.0 technologies and creating social learning spaces.

Bob is the local area co-ordinator for information literacy with the Higher Education Funding Council (HEFC)-funded LearnHigher Centre for Excellence in Teaching and Learning (CETL). His role is to develop the learning area, produce research outputs and make available new resources to assist information literacy teaching. He travels extensively in Europe and the USA, delivering lecture programmes, developing links with library and information science schools and sharing good practice in information literacy with library instruction practitioners.

Susan Hornby

Susan Hornby has worked for the Department of Information and Communications at Manchester Metropolitan University since 1990. Her teaching and research interests are the education of information professionals, aspects of the politics and sociology of information, information in the health services, knowledge management and literature and its readers. Her publications include peer-reviewed papers in the areas of the information society, education for the professional information worker and information for health and knowledge management. She is co-author of *Simple Statistics for Library and Information Professionals* (LA Publishing, 1997) and co-editor of *Challenge and Change in the Information Society* (Facet Publishing, 2002).

Susan has served as a member of the Quality Assurance Agency (QAA) Benchmarking Panel for Librarianship and Information Management.

Calum Kerr

Calum Kerr received his BA in English and both his MA and PhD in Creative Writing at Manchester Metropolitan University, gaining the former in 1996 and the latter in 2005. He has had a number of short stories, poems and articles published in a variety of places and has taught Creative Writing in both further and higher education. He is currently taking time out from teaching to concentrate on his writing. His PhD work, *The Multiple Perspectives of Jekyll & Hyde*, can be found online at www.jekyllandhyde-multipleperspectives.co.uk. More about his other writings can be found on his website at www.calumkerr.co.uk.

Jane Mathieson

Jane Mathieson is Regional Co-ordinator of 'Time To Read', a pioneering partnership of reader development practitioners in public libraries across north west England. She was seconded to this position in 2002 from the Manchester Library and Information Service, which she had worked for in various capacities since 1984. Prior to that she worked for library services in Stockport and briefly in the London Borough of Bexley. Her professional interests are in sharing and developing enthusiasm for books and reading among staff and users, building partnerships and networks among library practitioners and providing advocacy for the region's literature and reading activities. Jane also currently chairs the board of Manchester Literature Festival, a position which marries professional and private enthusiasms.

Mike Mizrahi

Mike Mizrahi has been a key figure in academic bookselling in Manchester for over 30 years. His Portland Bookshop has been a key supplier of literature and textbooks to local universities, schools and hospital libraries for probably longer than any other supplier in the area. Mike knows a great deal about bookselling and has used all his skills to nurture and develop his business in the face of increased competition and changing reader requirements.

Francine Sagar

Francine Sagar has a BA in English Literature with History (2003) from Edge Hill College in Lancashire. Having moved to the UK in 1981 from her home in Chartres in France, she made her home near Southport, Merseyside. She taught French in a local secondary school for a number of years. Francine is very active in her community and has much experience in organizing and contributing to social groups, including book groups in particular.

Kay Sambell

Professor Kay Sambell has been researching and teaching children's literature for over 15 years. She currently works at Northumbria University, where she offers a range of courses on childhood, youth and literature on the BA joint honours course in Childhood Studies in the School of Health, Community and Education Studies. She has published widely on dystopian writing for young readers.

Kay was awarded a national teaching fellowship in 2002. She has a keen interest in enhancing students' experience of learning in higher education and plays a lead role in Northumbria University's Centre for Excellence in Assessment for Learning. She is Director of a national project (MEDAL (Making a Difference: Educational Development to Enhance Academic Literacy), http://medal.unn.ac.uk) which has launched a pioneering pedagogic network enabling academics and professionals to share good ideas about improving student learning in relation to the study of childhood, including children's and young adult literature.

Anne Sherman

Anne Sherman MA worked for Cheshire County Council for five years, as Reading Group Co-ordinator and Literature & Reading Development Officer, before her current appointment as Regional Reader Development Officer for MLA West Midlands. Her professional interests are in reading groups and mass reading initiatives, raising the profile of literature and reading development work within cultural services, and empowering frontline staff to deliver their own reader development initiatives. She sits on the Chester Literature Festival Committee and is a member of the editorial board for *Public Libraries Journal*.

Claire Warwick

Claire Warwick is Senior Lecturer in the School of Library, Archive and Information Studies at University College London. She is Programme Director of the MA in Electronic Communication and Publishing, and teaches modules on electronic publishing and its legal and social aspects and XML.

Her research is in the area of digital humanities, particularly in the development and use of electronic texts and digital libraries. She is also interested in the social impact of publishing technologies, especially the internet. She was principal investigator for the LAIRAH ('Log analysis of use of internet resources in the arts and humanities') project, and is a co-investigator for the UCIS (User Centred Interactive Search) project and an associate director of the VERA (Virtual Environments for Research in Archaeology) project. All study the implementation of digital resources and libraries for humanities users. She is also a member of the HCI

(Human–Computer Interaction)-Book Research Cluster (based in Canada), which is researching various aspects of e-book development and use.

She is Head of the Cultural Informatics Research Centre for the Arts and Humanities at University College London, and serves on the advisory boards of several digital humanities research projects. These include the Catalogue of English Literary Manuscripts, Bloomsbury and Reform in the 19th Century, and Treble-CLEF, an EU-funded project on best practice in digital libraries for cultural heritage. She is a member of the executive committee of the Association for Computing in the Humanities, and chair of the international programme committee for the Digital Humanities conference in 2009.

Introduction

This book is about all aspects of literature in relation to the reader. It covers the relationship between author and reader, and the impact that changes in technology and organizational and governmental policy have had on the publishing and promotion of literature. It reflects on the challenges facing library and information professionals in reader development, and examines current promotion and partnership options. We hope that it gives experienced practitioners, new professionals and students a firm underpinning knowledge on which they can build.

This is an essential guide *by* current practitioners *for* current practitioners and students. It is not intended as a replacement, but rather as a complement to, and development of, other texts, containing new ideas and practical advice for the modern information professional.

This is a guide to how readers develop, and the impact that they can have on what libraries offer. Implicit in the text are the questions: 'Who is the reader? How do we reach readers? What are the benefits?' The contributors offer chapters of an impressive range and scope, and there are some unconventional approaches to the topics. To link them together we have included a specific introduction to each section and a contextual preface for all chapters.

We believe that the varying voices and styles of the contributors will create a refreshing and involving reading experience. At times the tone is academic and formal; at times it is colloquial and informal: this reflects the subject and style of each individual. Our contributors include academics, a poet, a crime writer, a teacher, a bookseller, a hypertext creator and web page designer and, of course, library practitioners. Each brings a particular tone and perspective to the topics they develop. Every contribution includes a practical framework of examples for the reader to take away and put into practice in their own professional area. We see the book not so much as a jigsaw puzzle but as a mosaic: each of the sections can stand alone but read together they form a complete picture.

The book is divided into five sections exploring various connections between the author and the reader; it commences with a chapter written by an author and ends with a personal perspective from a reader:

Section 1 - Foreword: the author as reader
Section 2 - Reader development: promotions and partnerships
Section 3 - Works of imagination
Section 4 - Future directions
Section 5 - Afterword: the reader as author.

We would like to thank all our contributors for their time and expertise, and hope that you enjoy the result.

Susan Hornby
Bob Glass

Section 1

Foreword: the author as reader

Introduction: Section 1

In this section, Ann Cleeves explains how she takes an idea for a story, works with it, creates the manuscript, liaises with agent, editor and reader, and then promotes the work to her readers. This is a fascinating insight into how an author takes the writing process from idea to publication and beyond.

This chapter is of great value to library and information professionals as it provides a unique perspective on the world of the writer and her public. An understanding of this process will help inform and consequently underpin many of the reader development activities undertaken by practitioners.

Chapter 1

The imaginative spark

ANN CLEEVES

Editors' preface

This contribution presents detailed insight into the activities of a successful working author. Ann describes the process of writing from inception to publication, and provides a fascinating overview of the links between author, publisher, libraries and readers.

Introduction

In this chapter I consider how reading influences the process of writing – from the way the stories we read as children feed into our adult experience of the narrative, through to the editing, reviewing and promotion of a finished book. I explore the development of a book from original idea to completed manuscript, using two of my crime novels as examples, and then describe how the writer must be both author and reader during the editorial process. I look at the other professionals in the publishing industry – agents, editors and publicists – and suggest that a passion for reading is as important for them as it is for the writer. I consider the importance of the public library system in developing and promoting both new and more established writers, and suggest that librarians and publishers should make more effort to understand the other's role. Writers now understand the need to engage more directly with their readers, and I explore the way some authors come together to bring their work to reading groups and festival audiences. I use the Harrogate Crime Writing Festival as an example of good practice. The range of reading groups is considered and the potential of new technology in the promotion of books is discussed. I explain that at last publishers have come to recognize the importance of the reader.

In the beginning

First of all, I'm a reader. I understand how fiction works, what makes a good story and how to get inside a character's head, because I've always been absorbed by the books I read. I don't analyse what I read from a writer's perspective; when I'm reading, I'm lost in the story like everyone else. The process of writing is instinctive and develops naturally. We all know how to structure a joke. Standing at the bar, a beer in one hand, we string our listeners along, pausing just before the tag line for dramatic effect. Nobody's taught us how to do that. We've just heard enough jokes to know how it's done. The same goes for writing fiction. The more widely we read, the more we develop a feel for the best way to develop a plot.

I did 'A' level English and went on to read literature at university - although I dropped out in my second year. I'm not sure that much of the fiction I read academically has influenced my own writing. Something about all the probing for meaning and context seemed to inhibit the flow of the narrative and distance me from the process. Reading at its best has been an escape for me. I love to enter completely different worlds and to be carried along by the action. I really don't care what the writer meant to convey. I'm a selfish reader; I'm interested in my own relationship with and experience of a book. I like to hear what other readers have made of the same title, but only after I've finished it myself.

Like many contemporary crime writers, I started out with Enid Blyton - the detective stories, not the soppy school books. There was something compulsive about the adventures. I didn't care at all about the characters; I just wanted to know what was going to happen next. Then I moved on to Malcolm Saville. His writing was a revelation. Not only was there a pacy plot, but the books had characters I wanted to get to know better and a tremendous sense of place. In my teenage years I found Conan Doyle, G. K. Chesterton's *Father Brown* stories, then the 'Golden age' crime novels of Christie, Sayers and Allingham.

And all this time I was writing: dreadful bits of verse, stories to bore my sister and impress my teachers, and an angst-ridden diary. It was when I dropped out of university that I started my first novel. It had literary pretensions, and if I'd ever finished it, it would have been very short. Luckily the reader in me brought the writer to her senses. Would this be a book I'd actually want to read? Pay good money for? Carry home on the bus from the library? Absolutely not. I'd read the first page and the blurb and decide I didn't want to touch it with a barge pole. The books I read for pleasure, my comfort books, were all about crime. So why not try that form as a writer?

Completing the first novel

It was several years before I plucked up the courage to start a new novel. I'd met my husband, discovered Shetland and the Russian novelists, and still came back to reading crime when I was miserable or ill. Then we moved to the tiny tidal island of Hilbre. My husband was warden of the local authority nature reserve there. We were the only residents; we lived in the old telegraph house without mains water or electricity. At the time I was at Liverpool University, training to be a probation officer, and one of our assignments involved writing a dissertation about a sub-culture. Other people looked at groups relevant to social work. I chose twitchers, the obsessive bird watchers who collect the names of all the rare species they have seen. It generated quite a bit of interest in our seminar group, and I had the germ of an idea for a novel.

I didn't start writing properly until I'd given up work. I did write some scenes, and thought a lot about the characters, while I was preparing social enquiry reports for the Merseyside Probation Service. And my work as a probation officer gave some great insights – not just into the criminal justice system, but also into the lives and relationships of people I might not otherwise have met. Then I became pregnant, and decided a commute across several miles of mud and sand wasn't really much fun – and at last I had time to complete the book.

A Bird in the Hand (Cleeves, 1987) owed a lot to my reading of 'golden age' mysteries. It had an amateur sleuth as its central character: an amateur sleuth with a double-barrelled name and an Oxford education. I hadn't met many people like that in the council estates of Birkenhead, but thought that detective stories all had rich and usually aristocratic heroes. It was only later when I started reading more widely – the wonderful Resnick novels of John Harvey, and the hugely entertaining Rebus books by Ian Rankin – that I realized crime novels could be rooted in a real landscape and explore in a more digestible way the themes I'd identified in other literary works.

The writing process

Everyone writes differently. I have friends who plot out a book entirely in advance. They know what will happen in each chapter before they start the business of telling the story in the best way they can. For me, though, the process is more organic. The book develops from one scene and often starts with a theme rather than an idea for a plot. I don't plan at all, and although I do spend quite a lot of time brooding before I begin the first chapter, I'm thinking about abstract things like mood and voice rather than about the plot. In fact, in my sort of detective novel the plot rather takes care of itself. There's a murder, a limited number of suspects and a resolution. That structure allows me to devote my imagination to the strands of the book I enjoy most: the development of character, the relationship between people and place, and the unsettling nature of much family life. My books are surprisingly quiet and domestic. Perhaps this process will make more sense if I explain the genesis of my two most recent books: *Raven Black* (Cleeves, 2008) and *Hidden Depths* (Cleeves, 2007).

Raven Black

I've been asked many times where I got the idea for *Raven Black*. As this was the book which won the Crime Writers' Association's Duncan Lawrie Dagger crime fiction award, it's attracted the most attention. It began as a single scene. My husband is still a keen bird watcher and at that time there was a very rare coot on a loch in Lerwick, Shetland's main town. My Christmas present to him was a trip to see the bird. We did it as a day trip – 13 hours overnight on the ferry from Aberdeen to Lerwick, ten hours on the island, then an overnight trip back. It was between Christmas and New Year and there was very little daylight. After we had seen the bird, some friends took us out for the day. It had snowed and frozen very hard on top of the snow. There was even ice on the shore. The light was very clear once the sun came up. We saw three ravens, black against the snow. I thought if there was blood as well it would make a magnificent first scene.

That was all I had to work on. The image came from the fairy stories I'd read as a child. Snow White and Sleeping Beauty had skin as white as snow, hair as black as ebony and lips as red as blood. I was already working on a novel and thought I might turn the Shetland idea into a short story. Then I was invited back to Lerwick to run some events for World Book Day, and the idea took hold. I talked to some people, including a local ex-cop. By the end of the visit I was hooked.

The themes grew out of the place. I'd spent two seasons on Fair Isle but knew that however long I lived there I'd always be an outsider. I was interested in what constitutes belonging. I made my central character a Fair Islander, but of Spanish descent. There is a wreck of an Armada ship off the isle and, in my fiction, Inspector Jimmy Perez's ancestor was a survivor of that ship which is called the Gran Grifon. Does a man whose family has lived in Shetland since the 16th century belong there, even if he has a Spanish name and a Mediterranean appearance? What about a teenager who grew up in England, but who has made her home there? Or an elderly man who crofts the land but has never quite fitted in?

Hidden Depths

Hidden Depths was less serendipitous and more contrived in its inspiration. I wanted some strong visual scenes to start off the action. The idea of water and flowers creating a sense of theatre around the crime scene appealed. Then I had to consider what sort of person might commit murder in that way. At the same time I was interested in writing about a woman who has devoted her life to her family and feels in middle age that she deserves her own secret pleasure. The model for the woman and her marriage was Mrs Ramsay in Virginia Woolf's *To the Lighthouse* (Woolf, 1927). Mrs Ramsay holds the show together, entertaining her husband's friends and massaging his ego. There is no question that she will betray him, although she probably sees her realization that he is not the great man she has always believed him to be as a betrayal in itself.

I started off by liking Felicity Calvert, the Mrs Ramsay figure in *Hidden Depths*. Her husband is a self-important, self-obsessed man and Felicity looks after him. She is kind to the crew of friends he has gathered about him. She can throw a good party. However, later in the book I came to despise her. She needs the admiration of her husband's friends. Her turning of a blind eye to her husband's faults leads to violence.

You see that now I talk about Felicity as if I were a reader, not her creator. Throughout the writing process the author becomes a reader to check that the book is working. We ask the questions the readers will ask. What will happen next? Why did that person do that? Does that really make sense? And so the action moves on. And, like a reader who comes to the book for the first time, our sympathies shift.

The editorial process

Once the book is finished it's important to leave it for a while before coming back to it with a reader's eyes. If I'm too close to it I make assumptions: because I see a scene very clearly in my own head, I assume the reader can see it too, even if I haven't passed on the one small detail which might bring it to life. This last read-through before the book goes to editor or agent is vital. I read it very quickly, usually in one sitting, to check that the structure works and that there's sufficient pace. Sometimes awkwardness of phrasing jumps out even though I've already read it many times before. Often the scenes I thought most clever - the tricksy flashback in the second chapter - are the ones that need to be cut.

However, the distance I've created by setting aside the book for a while is illusory. I know these characters too well to read about them dispassionately. I know what's going to happen next. And that's why the roles of the agent and the editor are so important. I might discuss the ideas for a book with my agent and publisher in vague terms before I start writing, but I make a point of never describing work in progress. They need to come to the novel without preconceptions. I think they should read a novel first as if they'd picked it from the shelf in search of a good read. They should be prepared to lose themselves in the story. Only later should the commercial imperative kick in.

The relationship between author and agent is delicate and intimate. Your agent knows how much you earn, and has seen the rejections and the bad reviews. Agents negotiate business contracts, and are there to celebrate successes and commiserate after disappointments. My agent is the first person to read my books. I wait for her response as keenly as I do my publisher's. I value her judgements and consider all her suggestions about character and plot seriously. She is, after all, a professional reader.

I have been fortunate throughout my career in my agents. I hear terrible stories about writers who feel under-valued, betrayed and lied to. I have trusted both of my agents implicitly to act in my best interests. I acquired the first by chance, through the recommendation of a friend after *A Bird in the Hand* had already been accepted for publication. Murray Pollinger was one half of an exceptional partnership. His wife Gina represented most of the most celebrated writers for children in the country, and Murray had contacts with publishers throughout the world. When he retired I was transferred to his assistant Sara, who in time set up on her own. I know absolutely that Sara is on my side. Her criticisms are to make the books better. She battles for every translation deal, and her network of associate agents – in the US and Europe, and to deal with film and TV rights – is outstanding.

The role of the editor is always slightly more ambiguous. The editor is employed by the publisher, not by the author. A good book is not always a marketable one – at least, that is how it seems to some writers. And an editor is not a free agent. She (or he) might believe passionately that your book deserves a six-figure advance and a huge marketing budget, but it isn't in her power to provide it for you. Inevitably, she reads your book with different eyes. Even if the book has been commissioned, so the publisher has a commitment to take it – and I'm in that fortunate position now – it must be hard for her to lose herself in the story. She has so many things to think about. How will this title fit in with the rest of the publisher's list? How will she sell it to the marketing people? What sort of branding should they go for? What sort of jacket?

And yet having a supportive editor can make a huge difference to an author, both creatively and in the practical business of profile raising. I'm remarkably free of cynicism after 20 years in the business. I've trusted the editorial judgement of the majority of my editors; they've been enthusiastic, literate and often powerful advocates within the publishing house. *Raven Black* entered the consciousness of a lot of people simply because my editor talked about it to whoever would listen. She was honest enough before I signed the contract to say that there would be little marketing budget – my previous sales couldn't justify it. However, she said she would do everything she could to bring it to notice. And she did. She e-mailed the first chapter to every rep in the company, talked to sales managers for Canada and Australia and brought it to the attention of the person responsible for submitting books for prizes.

When giving feedback after reading a new novel, a good editor is honest about the flaws but aware that this is a desperately insecure time for the author. After spending a year with a book most writers are ready to move on to the next project. They don't want to spend time responding to pages of detailed suggestions, and even the most minor criticism can seem like a personal insult. It can't be an easy job to keep the writer on board, yet the editorial process must be collaborative. It must be very difficult to suggest to a famous writer, especially one who generates lots of income for the publishing house, that his (or her) script is less than perfect. I'm certain that my books are much better after my editor and I have worked on them together and I appreciate her tact and attention to detail. It seems unfair that the creative input of editors goes largely unrecognized.

The big day: publication

As publication day approaches, publishers often produce proof copies, which go out to reviewers and buyers for the major retail chains. Reviewers are unlikely to use limited newspaper space to slate books, unless they've been hugely hyped in advance or are by big-name authors, so any comment is usually positive and a great boost to confidence. I'm not sure how many people go out to buy books in response to a small review in *The Observer* or *The Times Literary Supplement*, but good notices make a difference to an author's standing within a publishing house. A glowing phrase can be selected to go on the front of the paperback edition. Scouts for foreign publishers can pick them up, and translation rights can boost an author's income considerably, even if the individual advance is relatively small.

Then comes publication day. There is a launch, if you're lucky or willing to organize it for yourself: cheap wine in a local bookshop and an audience of friends and family bullied into attending. Before I was published I imagined launch parties as magnificent occasions – champagne and canapés and queues of fans waiting to have books signed. The reality has never lived up to the dream, and recently I've arranged to launch my books in libraries. The Shetland launch of *Raven Black* was a joy, thanks to the great staff in Lerwick Library. My editor flew up from London to join us and we used actors from the local youth theatre to provide authentic voices for the readings. For me it was a chance to catch up with old friends – a couple had come from Fair Isle for the event. For the library, it provided an opportunity to attract new readers and to present a different image to the community.

Libraries and why we love them

Publishers have only just come to realize the potential for sales and for raising the profile of their authors through libraries. Even in recent times, there's been woeful ignorance about what goes on there. If more publishers actually became library members instead of relying on review copies and freebies for their reading material, perhaps the status and funding of the public library system would improve. If people who can afford to buy books now don't join their local library, when they're old or poor there won't be much of a service for them to enjoy.

I have the impression that libraries are also under-valued by publishers in the US. A couple of years ago I visited Malice Domestic, a huge crime convention held every year in Washington DC. Because I was interested in how reader development worked in the US, I arranged a visit to a library in Arlington, near the conference hotel. The staff were enthusiastic, committed and full of ideas. They organized a number of reading groups for people of different ages, interests and ethnic backgrounds. Their readers would have been fascinated to meet the authors at the convention and attend the discussion panels. However, nobody had invited them or even thought to tell the library that it was happening. The result was that most of the sessions involved writers talking to other writers: no new readers and not many sales.

A friend and best-selling author has a similar complaint: 'Each time I visit America I'm sent on the circuit of specialist bookstores. I meet the same readers every tour – and they would have bought the books anyway. Why don't they fix up some visits to libraries, so I could develop a new readership?'

Author events work very well in libraries in the USA. In the 1990s crime writers Peter Lovesey, Liza Cody, Paula Gosling and Michael Z. Lewin took an entertainment called *Murder We Write* on tour there. They're all great performers and they must have pulled in a new audience for their books. My husband and I stole their idea and put together an illustrated talk called *Murder on the Wildside*, taking a look at the places which have influenced my writing. We travelled round Massachusetts with a box of books in the boot of our hire car and spoke in nature reserve visitor centres, bookshops and libraries. Readers like the fact that a writer makes an effort to meet them. And, on a practical note, libraries usually pay fees! I sold a lot more copies than I would have done at a regular bookshop signing.

The attitude of publishers to libraries has changed dramatically in the past few years. There are still misconceptions and false expectations, but there's a new realization that library staff have enthusiasm, product knowledge and a passion to promote a wide range of titles. Without libraries there would be a tiny market for first-time authors, short fiction and novels in translation.

New partnership projects have developed. For example, Kirklees Libraries regularly invites sales managers from Pan Macmillan and Bloomsbury to meet librarians and the reps pitch new titles to them. This has worked well on both sides. Librarians pick up proof copies and learn more about how the industry works. Personal contact means that they hear in advance about which authors will be on tour in their area, and the first-time novelists who would be delighted to talk to reading groups – even without a fee. Publishers have a more realistic view of the potential of the library market, and the scope for promoting books and authors who would never find a place on the shelves of the major retailers. A planned pilot project will develop this approach in the north east of England.

Engaging with readers

In my experience most writers like engaging with their readers, and even if they're shy and reclusive they can see the value of developing a discussion with them. Until recently the only way a writer would meet readers was at a literature festival or a bookshop signing. Literature festivals can be intimidating for the general reader and for the writer, and there's nothing more depressing than sitting in front of a pile of books in a shop, watching customers who are determined not to be persuaded to buy scuttling past.

Now, perhaps because libraries have made a determined effort to bring writers and readers together, there is greater opportunity for engagement. The expansion of reading groups has meant that reading has suddenly become a more social activity. People are happy to talk about books. Things have moved on since a publicist told me that she was always being bothered by reading groups: 'Such a nuisance, darling!' Today, I think she'd realize that a reading group meant multiple sales and treat the organizer with more care. There are reading groups everywhere: workplaces, bookshops, bars and people's homes.

As part of the *Inside Books* project organized by the reader development consultancy Opening the Book, I have set up reading groups in two prisons. The response of the offenders shattered a lot of the stereotypes I'd held before I started. Some of the men in Preston Prison loved Meera Syal's *Anita and Me*, about a young Asian girl growing up in the West Midlands (Syal, 1997). The women in Low Newton Prison in County Durham were more predictable, bowled over by Chrissie Glazebrook's *The Madolescents* (Glazebrook, 2001). We arranged for Chrissie to come to the prison to meet the women, and it was a moving encounter for everyone concerned.

From the prison project I moved straight on to becoming reader-in-residence at the Cheltenham Literature Festival. The reading groups we set up there attracted quite a different set of readers, but they were equally enthusiastic.

In subsequent work as a reader development officer, I have been frustrated by the fact that there is no way to tap in to the reading groups who meet privately. We need a database of reading groups, so when an author is doing an event in a library we can send a personal invitation to every group in the area. Many library authorities organize readers' days – this is an informal festival of books which puts the reader right at the heart of the event. Every writer I know enjoys attending these events. It would be good to bring all the independent groups together to share enthusiasms and reading passions.

The internet has opened up communication between readers, and between readers and writers, in an exciting way. Some publishers are better than others at developing their websites and understanding what readers are after. Most authors now have their own websites with a contact e-mail address, and many writers' blogs talk about their favourite books as well as work in progress. One American reader recently e-mailed me to say she was part of an e-reading group with 800 members. The British Council has a reader-in-residence who facilitates an e-reading group with members from all over the world. When she was working for Kirklees Libraries, poet Rommi Smith started an online group for lesbian, gay, transgender and bisexual readers. Again, it would be terrific to have a database to make it easier to find a group to suit the individual. It's hard to know where to start, otherwise, especially for the techno-phobe.

Writers as performers

Most poets understand the importance of performance. Novelists find the process less natural – how can a small piece read aloud convey the flavour of a work 300 pages long? Recently, though, groups of writers have come together to take their work into libraries, colleges, festivals and bookshops. I belong to a group called *Murder Squad*. Since forming seven years ago we've been imitated, and now a number of bands of crime writers travel around the country promoting their books and the genre in general. Recently a group of fantasy writers have done the same thing – they go by the wonderful title *The Write Fantastic*! And a group of literary writers in West Yorkshire have toured with a performance called *Four Fathers*.

Murder Squad was the brainwave of Wirral crime writer Margaret Murphy. Her novels were getting good reviews, but these weren't being translated into good sales. Like other mid-list authors, she found that her publishers had a very limited marketing budget for promoting her work. So she pulled in six other crime writers who lived and worked in the north of England, and the group was formed. We've put together a brochure – three editions now – and have published an anthology of short stories and recorded a CD. Mostly, we get out to where readers are and talk about the deadly pleasures of crime fiction. There are several benefits to being part of a co-operative like *Murder Squad*. Writing is a lonely business and it's great to have the support of other members. I particularly value the advice of Martin Edwards, who edits the annual Crime Writers' Association anthology, when I'm writing short stories. And it's much easier to turn out to a gig in a bookshop or library with a friend. Apart from anything else, there's someone to go to the pub with afterwards.

The Harrogate Festival

In 1999, during the National Year of Reading, I was appointed reader-in-residence for three library authorities in the north east, and since then I've been straddling the worlds of reader development and writing. These interests come together brilliantly at the Harrogate Crime-Writing Festival. Harrogate is different from anything that's happened before in the UK, or perhaps in the world.

America has crime conventions, where readers and writers get together in the same hotel, share meals and drink together in the bar. To be truthful, most of the people there are either writers or aspiring writers. That doesn't make the event less enjoyable, but an awful lot of self-promotion goes on, and even during the panels the discussion can be sacrificed to authors plugging their latest books. The UK doesn't go in for conventions much, except in the worlds of fantasy and horror. Here we have literature festivals instead, and they're a bit different. Authors are still plugging their books, of course, but they're slightly more subtle about it. And because an author has to be invited to attend a festival – and can't pay to appear on a panel – there are fewer writers around. There's probably some socializing with readers at the end of the day, but it's not like a convention where everyone's staying in the same place.

Harrogate brings the best of both institutions – convention and literature festival – together. The festival is held in an hotel, so writers and readers can meet up in the bar, and occasionally go straight from there into breakfast. There's the same buzz of shared experience you get at a convention. However, authors are invited to attend well in advance and are even paid a fee. Competition to appear is fierce, so the panels are usually well prepared and interesting. Since the Harrogate Festival started I've been reader-in-residence there. My role has been to bridge the gap between local readers (and readers from all over the world who join us) and the festival.

The run-up to the festival in July usually sees me out in the community. I've run writing workshops in local schools, hosted a murder mystery in village halls, travelled with mobile libraries to talk about visiting crime writers and (my favourite) set up reading groups in pubs in the Dales. The aim of this activity is to encourage local people to come to the festival proper. They don't have to be there for the whole weekend – it's possible to book for a single event. And we've developed the tradition of a Saturday lunchtime reading group. This is a free session for readers only. Authors are welcome, of course, but only as readers and not to talk about their own books. Each session has a theme. We've done European crime in translation, short fiction, and books by independent presses. In the first year a dozen people turned up; last year there were 80 of us and we had to split up into four groups. In 2007 we returned to look at 'golden age' crime fiction and its influence on contemporary British detective stories.

Conclusion

So, reading is where I started, and the celebration of reading is still a big part of my life. It informs my writing, and when I get together with friends we talk about books, and it provides part of my income. There are worse ways to earn a living. There must be a close relationship between those who work in reader development, publishers and writers. We all share the same goal – to encourage a passion for reading and a more adventurous approach to promoting books. The declining choice in high-street shops means that libraries play a vital role in providing reading choice. It's in the interest of the publisher and the author to support this work.

Bibliography

Cleeves, Ann (1987) *A Bird in the Hand*, Fawcett.

Cleeves, Ann (2007) *Hidden Depths*, Macmillan.

Cleeves, Ann (2008) *Raven Black*, Macmillan.

Glazebrook, Chrissie (2001) *The Madolescents*, Heinemann.

Syal, Meera (1997) *Anita and Me*, New Press.

Woolf, Virginia (1927) *To the Lighthouse*, Hogarth Press.

Section 2

Reader development: promotions and partnerships

Introduction: Section 2

Section 2 considers the impact of recent and current reader development schemes and outlines possibilities for new projects. It commences with a discussion of partnerships in reader development, moves on to methods for making literature accessible to all, then discusses how one library authority's ideas on reader development changed over time. The section concludes with a very moving personal account of setting up 'Getting Into Reading', and the benefits to individuals and libraries of participating in such a scheme.

This section gives a wide perspective on the benefits to libraries, partners and individuals of participating in reader development schemes. It describes and evaluates a range of activities and provides an insight into the benefits and implications of setting up a scheme. It can also be used as a template for developing and evaluating new reader development activities.

Chapter 2

'Time To Read': the rise and rise of a regional partnership

JANE MATHIESON

Editors' preface

'Time To Read' is a pioneering regional network of reader development professionals in north west England. This chapter describes how the network and many of its projects and achievements were established. 'Time To Read' is a model of best practice in partnership working and there is much here from which people working in other regions can learn. The chapter discusses the effect that focused funding can have on reader development schemes, and demonstrates the value of establishing and maintaining networks of professionals and partners in reader development.

Introduction

Library authorities can form regional partnerships to co-ordinate reader development activity. This chapter will cover the development of north west England's 'Time To Read' (TTR) network, highlighting its role and achievements. It will take a chronological look at the work of TTR, picking out activities which demonstrate the value in working across local authority boundaries, and activities undertaken in partnership with external organizations.

TTR was the first regional reader development partnership to have a full-time, paid co-ordinator. The north west region that TTR covers is geographically large and includes 22 library authorities. It consists of the three large counties of Cumbria, Cheshire and Lancashire, and Greater Manchester and Greater Merseyside.

The early years of TTR

How did this unique development come about? The history is now quite lengthy. I shall try to describe it, giving a flavour of TTR's achievements over the years.

1996: the beginning

In 1996 Rachel van Riel of the organization Opening the Book[1] delivered a pioneering six-month training course in reader development and training to ten library authority representatives in north west England. This fired those attending with enthusiasm for reader development activity – much of which was happening already, but with little recognition from many library managers and often in the face of shrinking book and activity funds. Rachel helped the group to recognize the value of the reader in designing activity – starting from where the reader is rather than imposing a set of librarian values on our stock selection, promotions and events.

This training took place at a time when librarians on the lower and middle management rungs did not really meet their colleagues from other authorities, except at occasional conferences and training courses or by being active in a special interest group, which few people were. The team quickly recognized the value in continuing to meet, sharing ideas and potentially pooling resources to develop materials and activities from which everyone could benefit. So, from 1997 the group continued to meet to exchange ideas, with the permission of the Society of Chief Librarians in the north west (SCL NW).

1998: the National Year of Reading

The formation of the embryonic 'Time To Read' partnership was well timed, as 1998 was proclaimed the National Year of Reading and funding was made available for libraries to pilot experimental projects and activities to promote reading. The TTR team constituted itself, appointed a chair and treasurer, and invited other authorities to join. The fledgling team was joined at this stage by some keen new members who had been taking part in the Branching Out training programme,[2] also delivered by Opening the Book. Branching Out encouraged the formation of regional networks, to help cascade reader development messages nationwide.

Many authorities made individual applications for funding to develop short-term projects. At the same time TTR was well placed to bid for funding for a regional project, and seized the opportunity to demonstrate that working across authority boundaries could achieve something more ambitious.

The project that TTR developed for the National Year of Reading took the form of a cassette of book reviews, *Listen 'Ear*, aimed at housebound and visually impaired readers. Developed in partnership with the National Library for the Blind and with additional funding from the Ulverscroft Foundation, the product was carefully compiled, professionally produced and distributed around the region. Making the tape a reality involved addressing questions of tape production, copyright issues and, for the first time, distribution across the region.

However, this project had to be developed and delivered in addition to all other work happening locally. 'Time To Read' members, then approximately 14 in number, undertook this project in addition to other responsibilities in their home authorities. While the pooling of expertise, experience and, crucially, time and energy ensured the product came into being, inevitably some shortcuts were taken – a significant one being failure to address the marketing of the product to its intended audience. Naïvely, it had been hoped that access librarians (those in regular contact with visually impaired and housebound service users) would be keen to promote the tape to their users locally. Unfortunately, at this stage, the reader development message was not yet widespread and the team had not really explained what it was trying to achieve with the product. Some staff didn't fully appreciate its potential value, and therefore it didn't reach as many readers as it could have done with better word-of-mouth marketing. However the project team learned many valuable lessons from this exercise – the chief being the need to spread the word more widely about reader development ideas and principles.

1999–2001: two new projects

In 1999, following the success of the National Year of Reading, DCMS (Department of Culture, Media and Sport)/Wolfson funding was announced in order to try to help libraries generate more sustainable projects.[3] TTR was encouraged by SCL NW to bid for regional funds, and 14 authorities partnered in a successful bid for funding for a project entitled *Reading Lifelines*. Learning from the *Listen 'Ear* experience, the bid writers included an application for funding to pay for a full-time project co-ordinator, so that at least one person was sufficiently dedicated to the project. *Reading*

Lifelines, a project designed to target 16–25-year-old potential library users, appointed a regional co-ordinator from within the TTR team (Julie Spencer from Bolton Libraries, on secondment from her home authority).

After a largely successful year of activity, TTR submitted a second successful bid to DCMS/Wolfson for a second round of funding, announced in 2001. In all, 18 authorities partnered for the new project, called *Everybody's Reading*.

Reading Lifelines and *Everybody's Reading* were projects encouraging library use by hard-to-reach 16–25-year-olds, and employed a part-time outreach worker based in each partner authority. The projects centred on using information and communications technology-based and arts-based activities.[4]

These two projects, *Reading Lifelines* and *Everybody's Reading*, were key to the future sustainability of the TTR network. Project funding brought additional staff with new skills into library authorities, helped shift attitudes among existing staff and kick-started reader development activity in many places. Having a full-time co-ordinator enabled efficient management of the project, including budgetary control, in order to meet performance targets. Good practice was developed and shared regionally, and quality training provided. In addition, the co-ordinator worked with the main partners to achieve delivery of high-quality publicity materials and a first-class website. A small steering group supported the co-ordinator by offering advice, sharing the administrative load at meetings and training sessions and working on additional funding applications.

In addition, these projects demonstrated clearly that authorities benefited from working together towards common aims and objectives. Readers reached in one authority may have been small in number, but figures collected regionally provided evidence of considerable impact.

2002–2003: building on success

With DCMS funding due to come to an end, the Arts Council England North West (ACE NW) commissioned a consultation, and talked to chief librarians and reader development librarians about how the successful work in the region could be sustained and developed. This consultation recommended the appointment of a co-ordinator to take on a wider range of activity. The proposal was taken to SCL NW, and 19 authorities agreed to contribute funds to pay for a post. There was also generous start-up support from ACE NW. The post was advertised nationally and the new co-ordinator recruited (on secondment) in October 2002 for an initial two-year period.

The post was established with an open remit: to broaden the scope of reader development work being achieved in the region and ensure that reader development remained high on all library authority agendas. Once in post the co-ordinator needed to define more closely the specific aims and objectives, and translate these into actions which would be of value to the network.

With the help of MLA NW (Museums, Libraries and Archives North West), who early in 2003 had created a Libraries Development Officer post, the following aims were written into a business plan:

- to ensure best value by spreading innovative ways of delivering core reading-related services
- to develop new ways of regional working at a time of increasing importance of the regional agenda
- to provide practical benefits in terms of shared costs of training and publicity materials
- to obtain new funding from outside the library sector
- to raise the profile of libraries and reading with other agencies operating at national and regional levels
- to spread and share passion! – passion for the quality of services, and for the pleasure and value of reading – for both customers and staff.

Over the course of the first year, the co-ordinator strengthened the network by clarifying the value of meetings, introducing regular visiting speakers and establishing a website. This helped in the sharing of best practice and would be a useful source of information for network members, as well as showcasing projects and developments more widely. The network identified training priorities and started work on a regional reader development strategy. In 2003, the end of the first year, all 22 authorities in the region had come on board and agreed to contribute funding.

Recent TTR reader development projects

Now let us consider projects delivered across the north west region's libraries over the past five years. They have been included here to demonstrate the increased range and quality of activity that can be delivered with the support of extra co-ordination and co-operation, as well as targeted funding.

Promoting poetry

One of the first requests network members made was that the co-ordinator should provide some materials which could be used on National Poetry Day.[5] At that time, only a few library authorities were using the opportunity of National Poetry Day to promote poetry books: many felt hesitant. The co-ordinator decided to use existing contacts and to capitalize on the regional focus of the network. A number of poets based in the region were approached to provide poems that featured locations in the north west. These poems were then worked into beautifully designed posters and postcards. Ten colourful posters and accompanying cards were distributed to every library authority in the network, where they were used in a range of ways to enhance poetry book displays in libraries, town halls, staff canteens, schools, colleges and parks.

In addition, the co-ordinator extended the reach of Manchester's then Poetry Festival and helped to co-ordinate open mic sessions in six town centre shopping areas on National Poetry Day itself. This was the first time that many of the audience had witnessed the broad appeal of live poetry. One particularly successful event in Warrington town centre led to the formation of a regular live poetry group, which still meets and has organized further well-attended public events.

The promotion of poetry continues. Many more authorities now organize events on National Poetry Day. The TTR co-ordinator works to bring new poets from the region to the attention of librarians, and information about new regional poetry books is circulated and featured on the TTR website.

In 2006 a Poetry Book Crossing activity was organized. Book Crossing is an online scheme which emerged from the USA. People with books they would like to pass on to others can download a label and a registration number from the Book Crossing website.[6] These are placed into individual books which are then left in public places for others to find. Finders can then enter comments about the book on the website using the unique reference number, and journeys made by books worldwide can be tracked.

For the TTR activity, Book Crossing labels were printed centrally, allowing room for the registration number and stating that books had been released by library authorities. Poetry books by regional poets were supplied to all 22 library authorities. These were to be registered on the Book Crossing website and released into community venues on National Poetry Day. Library staff were guided to leave books in places where people would have time to read them, e.g. cafés, hairdressers, waiting rooms, and so on. A few were sent 'on holiday' with members of staff.

Some very useful feedback was received from the Book Crossing website, which provided some evidence that this activity had achieved its desired aim of encouraging people to discover or rediscover poetry and urged them to visit their local library for more.

Readers' days

Much of the year from early 2003 to 2004 was taken up by co-ordinating and helping to deliver readers' days in various parts of the region. Readers' days are mini-festivals: one-day events at which readers have the chance to listen to and meet a number of writers as well as fellow reading enthusiasts. They generally include reading group-type discussions as well as talks, and the best readers' days send their participants away with goody bags, new contacts and information about further reading activities.

TTR wanted to test whether or not readers were prepared to travel beyond their local area for this sort of large-scale readers' event. Over the course of 2004, six readers' days were held. Although successful in their own terms, our conclusions were that only a few people are prepared to travel beyond their own local authority boundaries. Reader's days are also expensive in terms of staff time and energy. For one or two of the days, TTR trialled sharing the organizational workload across authorities, but even then a high degree of attention to detail was required to organize a safe, enjoyable and worthwhile event which would have lasting impact. Undoubtedly they are enjoyable for the people who do attend them and they help create a 'buzz' around reading. We have continued to organize occasional readers' days where opportunities to do so have arisen in partnership with publishers, or to fit with our own thematic promotions.

To share some of the learning from this experience, a toolkit was written up and placed on the TTR website to inform future event planning.[7]

Best practice book

Aware that the co-ordinator post could end in autumn 2004 and wanting to leave some legacy, TTR planned and delivered a best practice publication, *Time to Read: Examples of Reader Development Work from North West Libraries 2001–2004*, with the help of Grants for the Arts funding.[8] This updated a previous best practice book published by TTR as part of the National Year of Reading work in 1998, but was a much more detailed and colourful publication. The book included examples of reader development activity from every library authority in the region, all written to a template, describing projects briefly, quoting feedback from staff and readers and reflecting on strengths and weaknesses. One of the unusual features of the publication was that it presented tips for other authorities wanting to repeat the ideas.

The book was distributed widely across the region, and continues to be used by trainers wanting a tool to use in creative training sessions. It was also promoted nationally through reader development channels: more than 500 copies were sold to library authorities across the country. While an enormous undertaking in terms of production, the value in producing this book was immense. It gave each library authority a publication which showcased a piece, or pieces, of work they were particularly proud of, and demonstrated that individually they were contributing to a body of imaginative work across the region that was recognized and valued. The book provides invaluable evidence of work done in the region, and demonstrates the quality of print and production that can be achieved with pooled resources.

Working on a reader development strategy

In the summer of 2004 SCL NW agreed to fund the co-ordinator post for a further two years. The co-ordinator turned attention to consulting about and compiling a reader development strategy for 2005–2008 for the region. Eventually called *Readers For Life*,[9] the strategy document was intended to demonstrate clearly how reader development helps to deliver responses to 'Framework for the Future' (the DCMS ten-year framework for libraries) as well as other government agendas. It outlines a set of actions which all local library services can work towards, and over-arches local reading strategies. It exists for those authorities not able to produce their own strategy, or to back up and support locally produced strategies. *Readers For Life* was endorsed by SCL NW and adopted by all 22 authorities. Progress as regards the strategy was monitored every six months and an evaluation report was to be produced in 2008.

Promoting writing from the north west

Bearing in mind the strong support from ACE NW, TTR wanted to demonstrate its contribution to the regional literature scene and libraries' support for locally based writers. Thus TTR began work on a new promotion, *Here and Now – The Best NW Writing in NW Libraries.*

The promotion aimed to identify as much fiction set in the north west region as possible. These were to be books reflecting the contemporary region, so no historical sagas or titles more than ten years old would be included. The purpose of the promotion was to help promote the writers whose books are set in the region and who deserve a wider readership.

The co-ordinator identified a long list of books which was placed on the TTR website as a continuing resource and continues to be updated.[10] Local librarians were encouraged to check catalogues and purchase as many of the titles as possible for displays. A small team organized the design and production of a wide range of print materials including banners, show cards, postcards, posters, drinks mats and mouse mats, which could be used in libraries as well as in external venues. Additionally, the co-ordinator secured grant funding to enable at least one event with a NW writer to happen in each library authority in the region.

The print material was acknowledged to be attractive and useful to TTR members. The books seem to have had varying appeal in different parts of the region. While some authorities reported that the books did not issue particularly well, others reported remarkable success and continue to promote them. This is possibly partly influenced by how many new titles an authority was able to purchase. The print material was deliberately left undated, so it can be used until it is no longer fit for purpose.

Another successful element of this promotion was a focus on building relationships between writers and librarians. Two very successful networking days were held towards the end of 2005, funded by MLA NW. These brought together librarians from the TTR network with around 45 writers: poets one day and prose writers the other. These days included an outline of the challenges faced by librarians when organizing events, such as a frequent lack of good marketing departments and insufficient time and financial resources. They also showcased examples of good practice from some parts of the region, such as the Cheshire Poet Laureate scheme,[11] the Murder Squad performance,[12] and a 'speed dating' activity giving writers the opportunity to promote themselves and their work directly to librarians.

The sessions were considered so successful by both writers and librarians that two further days were held in 2006: one for a new batch of writers and the other for some of the writers from the first day to work further on how to promote themselves through libraries.

A key purpose of the networking days was to help to break down barriers between writers and library staff, in order to encourage more events in libraries bringing writers and readers together. This has been successfully achieved in many places, although libraries remain limited in terms of what they can do with the resources available to them.

Literary magazines

In 2005, TTR was approached by ACE NW to assist with meeting the aim of providing support for the range of independently published literary magazines in the region. There are currently around 30 different magazines featuring new writing, ranging in size, quality and readership. The Arts Council has a responsibility to support new writing, and one of the ways in which it does this is by offering financial support to many of the magazines that are seen to be fostering good quality new writing. Some of these magazines clearly struggle to reach a wide audience, and placing them in public libraries was seen as a useful way to publicize the magazines more widely.

Alongside TTR, another regional partnership called *Index* operates in the region. *Index*'s aim is to foster and develop excellence in the region's creative independent publishers and to help connect these publishers' writers, and their work, with readers both inside and outside the region. *Index* promotes itself, as well as a huge range of independent literature activity, through a website called *Literature North West*.[13]

Following ACE NW's offer of funding to pay for subscriptions to literary magazines for the region's library authorities, the TTR co-ordinator worked with *Index* to identify, source and set up subscriptions. Currently each library authority in the region receives one copy of each literary magazine available in the region, as well as some print materials to help promote them. Authorities have been encouraged to keep the titles together (rather than spreading them thinly), so that they have visual impact and to spread word of their availability to readers' and writers' groups.

Library subscriptions can make all the difference to a magazine's survival. The library project will also gather in some feedback about magazine popularity with readers.

The Big Gay Read

During the summer of 2005, TTR became involved with a project that quickly evolved into the most successful partnership to date.

Two library authorities, Manchester and Salford, had decided to start up new reading groups reading lesbian, gay, bisexual and transgender (LGBT) interest titles. Initial meetings had led to discussion reflecting on the *Big Read*, the BBC's list of the UK's best-loved books, and on how that list had failed to include any known gay writers.[14] A chance suggestion –'Wouldn't it be great to have a Big *Gay* Read?' – was seized on by the librarians present. They approached the TTR co-ordinator to discuss how likely it was that other library authorities would be interested in working with this idea, as clearly the more support the idea had the greater the chance of achieving sponsorship and external support.

The co-ordinator and the network quickly agreed that this was potentially an exciting idea which would give library authorities a reason to promote some titles they perhaps would not feel confident about promoting in isolation. There was security in being able to say that the promotion was happening regionally. And the project would address the reader development aims of broadening people's awareness of a range of writing and introducing new authors/titles, as well as demonstrating support for a particular community which has at times felt excluded from services.

Approaches were made to Bertram Library Services,[15] to find out if it would be interested in working with TTR, and to a Manchester-based gay and lesbian arts festival called Queer Up North (QUN), to assess interest. This promotion, more than any other to date, excited the external partners from the start.

Bertram was keen to offer support as the promotion provided both a way to establish a link with authorities they were not currently dealing with and an opportunity to promote an exciting range of books and materials nationally. Bertram staff hoped it would encourage the sale of books that might be hard to sell otherwise. QUN loved it as a way of getting books and reading included in its festival. It brought a new artistic dimension and also extended the reach and profile of QUN beyond Manchester city centre.

The project, as it developed, was largely managed by QUN. A list of 21 titles was chosen with input from reading group members, and a website was built. The vote for the nation's favourite queer novel was promoted nationally and gained a huge amount of press coverage, largely but not exclusively in the gay press. Posters, flyers and booklists were distributed free of charge to all library authorities in the north west, and sold by Bertram nationwide. Sets of titles to readers' groups were acquired from publishers and loans of these across the region were co-ordinated by TTR. Library authorities purchased sets of titles at discount prices and promoted them.

In addition, QUN programmed an exciting strand of literature events into their May 2006 festival, including one author event in each of the ten Greater Manchester library authorities (grant funding constraints prevented these spreading more widely). The highlight of these was the presentation to Armistead Maupin by Sir Ian McKellan of a trophy in recognition of winning the vote for the nation's favourite Gay Read. A capacity audience in one of Manchester's largest venues seemed a fitting tribute to the success of this promotion and partnership.

Many TTR members said that they felt that the Big Gay Read had given them an opportunity to promote titles they wouldn't have promoted otherwise, and to confirm that LGBT interest titles would be borrowed. Some new LGBT readers' groups were established and continue to meet.

A legacy of this promotion is that literature events continue to be included in the QUN festival.

This partnership model transferred to Merseyside, where a link with a gay and lesbian arts festival in Liverpool called Homotopia lead to events promoting LGBT books and writers in all the Merseyside library authorities during November 2007.

Current activity and future plans

In summer 2006 the co-ordinator post was renewed for a further two years to September 2008. All 22 authorities and MLA NW continue to contribute funds. Regular ACE NW funding has ceased, although it continues to support individual projects through Grants for the Arts applications.

TTR continues to plan at least one large-scale reading promotion per year. In 2007, it launched *Pure Passion*, a promotion of romantic reading. After the previous year's focus on a specific minority community, some TTR members commented that they wanted a mainstream project with which they could work. *Pure Passion* was a promotion of modern love stories, intended to be very contemporary in feel and to broaden readers' awareness of the different sorts of romantic reading available today. TTR distributed print materials inviting people to suggest their own favourite romantic novel, and invited readers to vote for their favourite romantic novel from a recommended list. This promotion built on learning from the Big Gay Read's website development and promotional activities.

This project was developed in partnership with the Romantic Novelists' Association, which is well aware of the role of libraries in providing an audience for its members' publications. Many romantic novelists enthusiastically offered their support, and attended and helped to deliver all sorts of events in the region's libraries during 2007.

The 2008 promotions include one called 'Literary Liverpool' which reflect Liverpool's year as Capital of Culture. Libraries have a significant role to play, offering access to information about Capital of Culture activities generally, as well as generating their own book-focused promotion. Also, 2008 is another National Year of Reading, this time with a specific family focus: TTR will undoubtedly want to seize the opportunities this offers, as it did in 1998.

Looking outside the region

To this point I have concentrated on describing work that TTR has generated itself through internal discussions. There is, of course, a wealth of external reader development activity generated by other organizations, which TTR members need to be aware of, engage with and support. TTR cannot ignore developments taking place nationally, particularly the work being carried out by the Society of Chief Librarians to deliver the Books, Reading and Learning strand of 'Framework for the Future'. TTR needs to ensure that national offers are incorporated into the work of all the NW region's library plans and strategies.

At the beginning of the chapter I described how TTR was largely begun through the encouragement and support of Opening the Book, a company which provides training and consultancy to library services. Contact with OTB and its sister company OTB Promotions Ltd continues to be maintained, reps attending TTR meetings from time to time to promote new products. OTB's contact with library authorities is currently chiefly through the Frontline training programme which many authorities have taken up.[16] The TTR co-ordinator also continues to spread the word about new OTB products and training offers.

The Reading Agency

The other major player in the reader development world is the Reading Agency (TRA), a charity which develops promotional offers for libraries nationally through major partnerships with external organizations such as the BBC and publishers. TRA works closely with the SCL, and has responsibility for delivering the books and reading aspects of 'Framework for the Future'.

TRA manages its own relationships with individual library authorities, often asking them to sign up their commitment to particular projects. TTR is able to support TRA by helping promote new offers and providing opportunity for discussion at meetings, and often by identifying individual authorities that can be approached by TRA for feedback or examples of good practice.

TTR has worked directly with TRA on the development of one or two of its promotions, particularly the *Got Kids? Get Reading* promotion aimed at families,[17] and currently on the *Reaching Readers* project.[18] TTR offers one point of contact within the region for TRA project managers requiring information or an overview of success factors.

TRA has built a strong ongoing relationship with the BBC, and has successfully demonstrated to the BBC how well libraries can promote campaign messages and reach community-based audiences. The TTR network has proved to be particularly useful in helping authorities work with the BBC *RaW* promotion. Standing for Read and Write, this is a current three-year BBC promotional campaign addressing literacy. Since 2005, *RaW* has provided ideas and materials to work with and occasional pots of funding for local areas. TTR has pulled together the appropriate local library staff to share ideas and information about their *RaW* activity. This has been useful to the region's BBC Learning Partner in providing an overview, and motivated local librarians to continue to work with the promotion. Increasingly, the BBC's Learning Partner in the region has liaised with TTR and provided local offers of materials and financial support for activities. Without TTR, *RaW* may have dropped off the radar of some authorities, although supporting literacy campaigns remains an important area of librarians' work.

Conclusion

The past ten years have undoubtedly seen huge growth in the number of offers made by external agencies and partners to libraries to assist with reader development. It could be said that by generating additional activity, TTR complicates the national picture and overstretches the resources of librarians in the region. Other regions manage reader development activity without a full time co-ordinator, but I would argue that in this region we achieve more and to a higher standard.

The fact that SCL NW continues to endorse the co-ordinator role is testimony to the value local reader development librarians feel they gain from TTR. Recent comments received from individual librarians, when asked what they consider the main benefit of TTR to them, cover the following:

- stimulating new ideas and reigniting enthusiasm and motivation allowing the exchange of ideas and the sharing of good practice
- helping them to engage with other authorities and wider reader development campaigns
- providing the ability to draw on a wide breadth of knowledge and experience and to gain support from the region
- assisting in achieving local targets and meeting local priorities
- breaking down isolation, and having fun.

The strength of the TTR network lies in the commitment of its members, who work in libraries and the community. It is they who enthuse and motivate other staff, encourage the formation of new readers' groups, address the presentation and display of stock, pick up and work with new national offers and promotions, and act as advocates for reader development with their managers and external partners. Network members encourage each other and share ideas generously.

The TTR co-ordinator continues to organize training courses in response to demand, consider how to monitor and evaluate activity better, and provide information to managers and ongoing individual support to TTR members when needed. While TTR members would ideally have the time to spend looking outside the region to developments elsewhere, it is inevitable that most energy is spent looking inwards to the region.

The north west's chief library officers are to be congratulated on having sustained their high level of commitment to reader development for so long. Learning from best practice elsewhere, the TTR network must strive to maintain its high standards of activity and the motivation and commitment of its members, and continue to be unafraid to try new ideas in its mission to extend existing readers' enjoyment of reading and to assist new readers in discovering and benefiting from reading services.

Bibliography

1   Opening the Book, www.openingthebook.com.
2   Branching Out, www.branching-out.net.
3   Museums, Libraries and Archives Council, www.mla.gov.uk/website/programmes/dcms_wolfson.
4   Time To Read, www.time-to-read.co.uk/toolkit_03.htm.
5   The Poetry Society, www.poetrysoc.com.
6   Book Crossing, www.bookcrossing.com.
7   Time To Read, www.time-to-read.co.uk/toolkits/toolkits.asp.
8   Caldwell, A. (ed.) (2005) *Time To Read: examples of reader development work from north west libraries 2001-2004*, Time To Read.
9   Readers For Life (2008) *A Reader Development Strategy for Public Libraries in the North West Region, 2005-2008*, Time To Read.
10 Time To Read, www.time-to-read.co.uk/read/.
11 Cheshire County Council, www.cheshire.gov.uk/readersandwriters/writers/poetlaureate/poetlaureatebecome.htm.
12 Murder Squad, www.murdersquad.co.uk.
13 Literature North West, www.literaturenorthwest.co.uk.
14 BBC, www.bbc.co.uk/arts/bigread/.
15 Bertram Library Services, www.bertramlibraryservices.com.
16 Frontline, www.branching-out.net/branching-out/page2.asp?idno=910.
17 Literacy Trust, www.literacytrust.org.uk/vitallink/gotkids.html.
18 The Reading Agency, www.readingagency.org.uk/projects/organizations/reading_partners.html.

Chapter 3

Reader development and social inclusion

LINDA CORRIGAN

Editors' preface

Since December 2006, all public sector organizations in the UK have had a legal duty to promote equality of opportunity for disabled people. Until libraries consider the needs of disabled people throughout their policy and planning for service delivery, as well as in facility provision, such equality will never be achieved. This chapter will focus the minds of anyone involved in service delivery, from senior management to frontline staff.

Introduction

This chapter will discuss bringing literature to all readers - to the whole community. People can be isolated from literature in many ways: physically by not being able to get to where books are; culturally by perceiving books and literature as not being relevant or accessible to them; or by being unable to access the printed word.

Addressing exclusion from literature

Physical and cultural exclusion can be addressed by adjusting the way libraries deliver services, by ensuring that libraries have an inclusive selection policy which is applied and by making sure that staff are trained to deliver services to excluded groups of people. Libraries also need to be particularly proactive and imaginative to make sure that literature reaches people who cannot access the printed word; the barriers to reading can be immense for this group. This chapter begins by examining exclusion from literature in general, and then moves on to the particular difficulties faced by people who are unable to access print. On the way, it will consider ways of addressing the need and will finish with some examples of good practice.

Literature and disability

Disability can both distance people from literature and bring them to it. There are obvious difficulties in accessing libraries and bookshops for people with physical impairments. For example, if walking is a problem, just the positioning of the library may make things difficult, if it is too far from bus stops or parking places. It might be so far away as to put off someone who is not strong, even if they have a wheelchair and the library has ramps.

Most library authorities seek to offset such difficulties by providing mobile services, but even these may not be accessible to the infirm or wheelchair users, depending on the modernity of the equipment. The best new mobile libraries have lifts which allow access for both wheelchair users and those who cannot climb steps, as well as online access to the library authority's full service. Even so, at best they offer browsing from a very limited range of the library's stock on a two- or three-weekly basis, on a timetable organized for the authority's convenience and heavily dependent on the reliability of staff and equipment. This is not meant to criticize the extremely good work done by a lot of authorities and staff. It is simply a statement of fact. However good the service is, and however grateful users are, it is still a poor substitute for being able to take your car or a bus and go to the library or bookshop, on a whim, to browse for whatever you want in the way of literature. And that is leaving aside the need to access information.

For those people who are unable to use the mobile library, the problem is even worse. They are reduced to relying on services for housebound people: books or tapes/CDs are delivered in batches or by post, usually following a genre selection often generated years before and long ago exhausted. Some of the recipients of these services may be relatively young, healthy carers who are simply unable to leave their charges during library opening hours. Others may be well-educated, opinion-forming people whose disability prevents them from accessing the kind of reading material that they require.

Other people may be prevented from accessing print materials for an assortment of reasons. People with arthritis in their hands may be unable to hold a book, particularly a heavy hardback, or may be unable to turn the pages or keep the book open. People with dyslexia may have a real interest in literature but be unable to read it for themselves. And then there are the people who find that their eyesight (or lack of it) creates an impenetrable barrier between themselves and the printed word.

Literature and diversity

It is the job of libraries to promote literature to the whole community, but some excluded groups fall into the gap between definitions of social exclusion and diversity, even though both might have been presumed to be all-encompassing. Indeed, in 1999 the Department of Culture, Media and Sport (DCMS) Policy Action Team (PAT 10) defined the overall aim of its social inclusion policy as: 'to promote the involvement in culture and leisure activities of those at risk of social disadvantage or marginalisation, particularly by virtue of the area they live in, their disability or age, racial or ethnic origin. To improve the quality of people's lives by these means.'[1]

This definition embraces a broad sweep of society, including people who live in areas of disadvantage, both urban and rural, disabled people, older people and people from racial and ethnic minorities. However, as the Chartered Institute of Library and Information Professionals (CILIP) Diversity Group has noted, it does not include refugees, asylum-seekers, travellers (who are not considered to be an ethnic minority), lesbians, gay men, bisexuals and transgendered people (LGBTs), people with basic skills needs or single parents.[2] Adding the two group definitions together, we come to the realization that, as library workers, we need to address the needs of a wide-ranging group of people who may be isolated or alienated from literature.

Multiple exclusion

As mentioned earlier, a fine line is often drawn between definitions of social inclusion and diversity services. It is my contention that the drawing of such a line is unwise. People in general do not fit very well into pigeon-holes. Just naming the groups in the list above is an attempt to pigeon-hole or label the people within them. However, people do not conform so willingly. A disabled person could belong to a minority ethnic group, live in rural poverty and/or be gay too. When addressing one aspect of a person's requirements, we should not ignore their other needs. Multiple exclusion is very real, relatively common and frequently underestimated.

Although I have thus far focused on the many ways in which people can be excluded from literature, it is also worth remembering that some excluding factors can also be instrumental in bringing readers to books. If I had £1 for every time that I've heard the sentence, 'I never used to read until I lost my sight,' I'd be a very rich woman. The same is probably also true for other disabilities and for other groups of people. Many people find that when one avenue closes to them, others open up. Visually impaired people often say that when they had their sight, they were too busy playing tennis, climbing mountains or enjoying some other hobby to have time for reading. This means that when some of them come to reading as a new leisure activity, they have a clean slate. They have no preconceptions about what kind of books they like. They are not in a very good position to find out what is on offer. As a result, some read voraciously anything which is offered to them in any form (audio, e-book, very large print, etc.). However, others are put off by some things they are offered and, in an attempt to avoid such disappointments, gradually narrow their parameters of choice until all they are left with is the bland and insipid. If ever there was a group of people crying out for someone to bring literature to them, this is it. But they are not alone. Many other groups also come to reading by default and need help to acquire the confidence to enjoy it. This is where libraries come into their own.

Bringing literature not literacy

The main theme of this book is 'bringing literature to readers' and it is a good idea to keep this in mind when we think about literature and social exclusion or diversity. It is very easy to become diverted from the path of literature towards bringing literacy to excluded groups. The whole literature and reader development movement, of which this book is a part, often gets sidetracked towards literacy projects – not least because it is often in this area that funding can be found.

This is not to say that literacy is not part of libraries' remit, or that literacy projects are not a good thing. The library has many roles to play in people's lives, and access to education (including literacy and other basic skills) and access to information are very important functions of library services. However, so is the function of supporting established readers in becoming confident, adventurous, outreaching consumers of the vast array of literature on offer.

Literature is an educator in itself. It is a route to understanding and tolerance of the world. Literature can provide travel for the homebound, appreciation of different religions and social practices for the isolated or the threatened, and even insight into sexual orientation for the timid or for those unable to observe the differing behaviours of people around them. It has a huge role to play in developing tolerant citizenship. Literature in translation has as large a role to play in developing understanding within the indigenous community as English literature does in demonstrating the social mores of this country to newcomers.

Print disability

The importance of appreciating the difference between literature or reader development and literacy development cannot be overstated. Neither can the importance of understanding the difference between becoming literate and gaining new language skills. The fact that a person cannot read English does not necessarily mean that they are not literate in another language. Being illiterate implies a lack of the basic skills needed to conduct life as an independent person. However, a person can be educated to well above basic skills levels and still be unable to access printed English.

A person who needs to read audio books may well be literate but no longer able to see well enough to read. They may be literate in Braille but seeking material not available in that format. Alternatively, they might understand spoken English better than written English or have a print disability such as dyslexia which creates a barrier between them and print rather than between them and literature. It is important to bring literature to all these members of society. Other programmes will bring literacy, and in the long term some readers will move from the group acquiring literacy into the group acquiring confidence with literature. The two are not mutually exclusive but they are not the same.

The reading experience

Let us now move on to examine the specific needs of visually impaired people, while bearing in mind that they may have other needs as well. Print disability is in many ways the hardest difficulty to overcome. People who have other physical difficulties or who meet social or cultural barriers to literature can, once they have made contact with the book or computer screen, access the material for themselves. This is not the case for visually impaired people.

A visually impaired person only has the same experience in relation to literature as a sighted person if they are able to read Braille[3] or Moon.[4] In all other cases someone or something comes between the reader and the material. With audio books, there is usually a human interpreter.[5] The presence of that reader immediately alters the context of the novel or poetry being read. The text no longer has the cadences and inflexions of the reader but, rather, of the interpreter. Just the sound of the voice of the interpreter reading dialogue can subtly change the reader's perception of a character from that which they would have formed without an interpreter.

It is now possible to read many books using a computer, with the text either magnified to the required size or with screen-reading software reading the text aloud. Screen readers use synthetic voices to read the text. Synthetic voices have improved immeasurably over the past 10 years, and no longer sound like the voice that we have come to associate with Stephen Hawking. In many cases they sound almost human. However, in this instance it is the flatness of the voice, the lack of inflexion and cadence, that can become a barrier for the reader. Certainly, no one has yet invented a screen reader that can read poetry.

In addition, there are all kinds of taboos around the use of particular words or expressions or descriptions of human activities which have a different effect if spoken aloud rather than read in the head. True, the availability of headsets now offers a degree of privacy, but many people find these uncomfortable to use and prefer loudspeaker systems. Such taboos might well militate against listening to *Trainspotting*[6] or *American Psycho*[7] on a loudspeaker system when anyone from your grandchild to the vicar might walk in.

Ways of addressing the need
Understanding the demographics

When libraries set out to address the reading needs of visually impaired people, to bring literature to them, they first of all have to meet all the physical requirements of the Disability Discrimination Act.[8] Potentially, there is much to be said about the difference between meeting basic needs and making a visit to the library a comfortable and rewarding experience – however, that is not the subject under discussion here. Libraries also have to move beyond the physical to ensure that their services are accessible and usable.

To provide accessible services, there must be an understanding of the needs of visually impaired people at all levels of the library staffing structure. There is little point in having frontline staff fully trained to provide accessible services if senior and middle management are coming out with plans and initiatives within which the needs of visually impaired people (or other alienated groups) have not been considered at all. This just leaves the counter staff having to exercise their initiative to palliate the deficiencies of the plans. Equally, there is little point in having senior and middle management fully on board as regards accessible services and inclusive projects if the frontline staff lack the confidence to work with visually impaired and other disabled people.

The starting point for accessible services is an understanding of visually impaired people in the community. Here, a few facts and figures are useful.

Visual impairment can range from the need to wear spectacles to complete blindness. It is usually defined as a sight deficiency which cannot be mitigated by the use of spectacles. There are no exact figures for the prevalence of sight loss in the UK, but it is believed that there are nearly two million people in this country with impaired vision (approx 1.7 m)[9] and that just under a million of those have serious sight loss.

> There are around two million people in the UK with a sight problem. This means that while wearing glasses they are still unable to recognise someone across the road or have difficulty reading newsprint. Among these two million people, over 370,000 are registered as blind or partially sighted. There could be an additional 20 per cent who are eligible for registration but have not yet done so.[10]

This failure to register can be a result of ignorance of the benefits of registration, but it can also be the result of a positive decision not to register. People cannot and should not be forced to register. Reasons for positive non-registration can range from denial to unwillingness to become involved with 'the authorities'. All of these are sensitive issues and need careful and considerate handling. The issue of registration/non-registration is one of the reasons for the approximate nature of all figures concerning visual impairment in the community.

According to the Royal National Institute of the Blind (RNIB), 100 people in the UK start to lose their sight every day.[11] In the UK sight loss is predominantly a condition of older age. Around 85% of visually impaired people are over the age of 65, but there are about 25,000 children in the UK with sight problems, 12,000 of whom also have other disabilities.[12] It is also believed that there is a large group of people, the RNIB estimates numbering four million, whose sight problems have not been identified.

> Evidence from Department of Health data show that it is highly likely that over 4m older people do not have their visual difficulties identified because they do not have regular eye examinations. This is in spite of the provision since 1999 of free examinations to those aged over 60.[13]

We are all used to the concept of the blind man with his white stick or the blind lady with her guide dog, but do we appreciate how much or how little they can see? According to the RNIB, 'Being blind does not always mean that a person is living in total darkness. Forty-nine per cent of blind people and eighty per cent of partially sighted people can recognise a friend at arm's length.'[14]

Something like 20% of people who are defined as 'blind' have such severe sight loss that they can only detect the difference between light and shade or even less. The remaining 80% have some useful sight. Some people may have only peripheral vision and no central sight. Others may have only central vision or patchy vision with blank and defined areas and others still may see things as a general blur. However, the relevant point is the importance to those 80% of 'well-positioned, easy to read signage, ideally with a tactile or Braille element',[15] as well as similarly accessible promotional literature and information.

At the last census (2001), for the first time there were more people aged over 65 than under 16. That is likely to continue and indeed become more pronounced in the UK over the next few decades. Given that almost all surveys of library usage show higher usage figures in the under-10s and the over-45s than in any other age groups, what does this say about the profile of visual impairment among library users?

The net result of understanding all the information given above should be an appreciation that visual impairment is a lot more common than we might think and that it is frequently a hidden problem. Furthermore, as a society - not just as libraries - we fail to take account, in signage and in so many other ways, of the useful vision that people do have.

Training

Here I return to my earlier point about the importance of training for all library staff. I did a lot of training of public library staff, at all levels, during the early 2000s. While for the most part this was a very rewarding experience, on occasion I have been reduced to despair.

In one particular exercise, groups were asked to try to imagine what it was like for a visually impaired person to enter one of their libraries. They were asked how easy it would be to find the issue or enquiry desk, whether or not a person working at the desk would be able to see and offer help to a person floundering inside the door, whether it was part of anyone's job to offer that help, whether a person with reduced sight would be able to navigate the library with accessible signs and where technology for enhancing print could be found. On more than one occasion, I was told that the members of the group couldn't do the task because they were managers and worked at headquarters not in a library. Can it really be the case that library managers never set foot in any of their branches? Can they really mastermind plans and initiatives without some understanding of how roll-out might differ in different branches? Should they be allowed to make plans without considering how they will be implemented at the front line?

It is important to remember that any library service is only as good as it is perceived to be on the day that the visually impaired person walks into the library. It may be an authority's policy for all staff to have visual impairment awareness training, and with luck it will be repeated on a three-year cycle along with manual handling training – but is it also part of induction training? If it isn't, for a period of anything up to three years a member of staff may be staffing the front desk with no training in how to address or help a visually impaired person.

Accessible services

When we start to think about accessible services, we have to think about just what services we mean. We have to have a starting point. In my view that starting point should be the view that visually impaired people should have access to the same kind of library services as sighted people. The services may have to be delivered slightly differently, but they should be the same kind of services, delivering a similar end result, and they should be of the same, not inferior, quality.

Technically, there is very little material in libraries which cannot be made accessible but members of the public, both sighted and visually impaired, are not aware of this and neither are the majority of library staff. As mentioned earlier, 80% of people registered as blind have some useful sight and those people who are registered as partially sighted also use their sight to a large extent. Of the people with very significant sight loss, only a very tiny proportion (around 12,000 and decreasing) read Braille. By far the majority rely on large print, audio materials, reading machines and closed circuit television (CCTV), all of which are available to a greater or lesser extent in public libraries.

A number of charities are working to provide reading material for visually impaired people. The newly formed RNIB National Library, a combination of the library services of the RNIB (including the Talking Book Services) and the National Library for the Blind, does sterling work in providing Braille, audio, digital and giant print books as well as Braille music and an interactive website including an OPAC (online public access catalogue). In terms of the provision of Braille, there will always be a need for specialist suppliers.

Dealing physically with Braille books is not feasible on a large scale for public libraries. However, most libraries do provide audio books and much else besides. They also fulfill a major function in the information and reading lives of the community. It is therefore a fundamental requirement for social inclusion that libraries should be providing services to the visually impaired people in their communities.

It really matters a great deal if visually impaired people feel that they have to go somewhere other than libraries (usually to charities) for their reading. First of all, it sets them apart from the rest of the community. It also means that they do not see all the notices on the board (even if they are accessibly designed), so they do not know what else is going on, they miss out on all the promotional activities, they do not bring their children or grandchildren to story-time and they do not join reading groups, because they do not know about them or do not think they will be accessible.

Libraries, along with many other public services, have been considerably exercised by the Disability Discrimination Act (DDA).[16] Much has been done to make library buildings accessible and to make sure that someone in the authority is responsible for overseeing services for visually impaired people. However, what has not been done, in many cases, is to use the opportunities afforded by the DDA to examine the reading needs of visually impaired people, to ask: what actually are these reading needs? When that question is asked, it seems to surprise a lot of the public and library staff that the reading needs of visually impaired people are exactly the same as those of sighted people. For visually impaired people, the reading material just needs to be provided in a different format. We mistake the person for the product. We define the reader by his or her preferred format (our large print readers or our audio book readers) rather than simply looking at them as members of the public who want to read just the same things as the rest of the public but who happen to have reduced sight.

Making stock accessible

Like everyone else, visually impaired people want to read the books that everyone is talking about: the current bestseller or the biography that's in the news at the moment. Alternatively, they may be forensic crime aficionados or have a hobby or interest which they wish to pursue in their reading. Often there are waiting lists in public libraries for the latest bestsellers, but for visually impaired people there may not even be an accessible format unless they are Braille readers or unless RNIB Talking Books or the Calibre Audio Library[17] happen to have made versions. However, for people with some usable sight there are alternatives.

Let us consider equipment first of all. Within almost every library authority in the UK there are CCTVs (hand-held and frame mounted),[18] scanners, large-screen PCs, screen-reading software (*Jaws* or *Supanova*),[19] magnifying software,[20] keyboard enhancement equipment (glove or stickers), magnifying glasses (hand-held or stand-alone), photocopiers for enlarging, dedicated reading machines (e.g. Kurzweil) and book stands to angle books to the light or for people who cannot hold books. Some authorities also have PCs with Braille display, Braille note-takers and organizers, Braille embossing facilities and voice recognition software.

Thus, technically, within each library authority the means are there for visually impaired people to read what they want. Typically, however, library staff direct visually impaired people (the ones they recognize) to large print and audio materials. At the same time, many visually impaired people concentrate on getting from the front door to the audio or large print material as safely as they can, because they know the way there.

Also typically, staff who are aware of the technology mentioned above complain that it is not used – that there is no demand for it. Other members of staff simply do not know that the technology is there, and the visually impaired people certainly do not know it is there or what it can do. You do not go up to the library desk and ask if there is a machine which will magnify text to letters 6 cm high (magnification software) if you do not know that such technology exists. Neither do you ask if there is a machine which will read text aloud if you do not know about such things (Kurzweil machines).[21] You most certainly do not see and recognize such technology if you are visually impaired and no one tells you about it – which brings us neatly back to the training issue.

All members of staff need to be clear and confident about using technology which will allow all visually impaired people access to books and services. They need to know about mouse pointer enhancement; changing the size and colour of onscreen fonts, the colour options available on the computer screen and adjusting accessibility options in Windows and Internet Explorer. All staff also need to know about the location of assistive technology, from the most basic to the highly technical – from magnifying glasses upwards. They need to know how it works, what it is useful for and where the instructions are kept.

Armed with this information, a member of staff can scan in the chapter of a book which someone wants to read and then set off the screen reader to read it. You do not have to be a technological wizard to do that much. Equally, a normal print book could be scanned in and looked at with screen magnification software if no CCTV is available. And remember that CCTV doesn't have to mean a big platen (flatbed) style machine: it could be a hand-held easy reader with a TV screen. What matters here is that staff should know how to use the CCTV or the scanner, and that they should be able to at least boot up *Jaws* or *Supernova* and set it off to read.

It is true that not all libraries have all the technology. Kurzweil machines are expensive and there tends to be only one per authority. However, they are portable and could be rotated round different branches on a schedule. Alternatively, schemes could be organized to enable visually impaired readers to visit the central library to use the technology. In addition, most branches have at least one or two PCs these days, and with blanket licenses for assistive software there is no excuse for not making it possible for visually impaired readers to read what they wish. Small-scale CCTVs are neither prohibitively expensive nor too large for even small branch libraries, and can even save staff time. Setting a visually impaired person up with a pile of audio books and a CCTV to allow them to read the blurbs for themselves is more satisfying for the reader who gets the browsing and choosing experience and releases a member of staff to assist someone else.

There must be dozens of people who go to the library every day to pick up large print books and would love to read much of the other material in the library if someone just pointed out to them that they could. Library staff members complain that they have brief instruction on the use of access technology and then do not get to use it for six months and forget what to do. The follow-up complaint is that there's no demand when actually the library has plenty of customers who need it: they just do not know it is there and the staff do not offer because they haven't been trained to think of either access technology or visually impaired people in the right way. They just see a narrow band of blind people instead of the great mass of people with a visual impairment.

Examples of good practice

The previous section of this chapter has taken us slightly away from bringing literature to readers, at least in part to demonstrate the practical ways in which this can be done. I want to return now to some examples of excellent practice in the area of bringing literature to visually impaired readers.

It may also seem that the previous section has created a fairly gloomy picture of the services provided for visually impaired readers in English public libraries. However, there has also been some very good work in the past ten years. Indeed, there have been far too many good projects for me to outline them all here. I therefore have no choice but to pick out just a few. Some of them are continuing initiatives and others have been more short term. The really sad part about all of the examples is their sporadic and fragmentary nature.

While much has been done to demonstrate successes where they have occurred, there has been a signal failure to take up these successes and replicate them around the country. There is a constant quest for innovative fundable projects, which raise expectations but cannot always be maintained once funding has ended. Innovation is not an end in itself. If an idea is good and it works in one part of the country, it is likely (perhaps with slight regional modifications) to work elsewhere. In essence, those people working on the original idea and project are conducting the pilot study for everyone else. However, project managers and funders alike continue to seek new ideas and repetitive pilot studies instead of taking advantage of tried, tested and successful methodologies.

In accessing literature, visually impaired people tend to face two main difficulties: accessing their reading material in a suitable format (as discussed in the previous section) and browsing and choosing books for themselves. Most of the examples I will give in this section address the browsing and choosing needs of visually impaired people.

Example 1: Essex reading groups, *Booktalk* magazine, book festival and Ask Chris website

Essex libraries probably run or have given birth to more reading groups than any other library authority in the UK: over 400 at the last count. Many of these reading groups serve an important social function in this large and disparate county, as well as bringing literature to readers and embracing readers who need to use alternative formats.[22]

In addition to the reading groups there is also a very healthy and accessible book festival held annually in the spring, and a *Booktalk* magazine which reached its 23rd issue in December 2006 and which ties together the reading groups and the festival. The magazine offers information about the festival and the reading groups, book reviews, author insights, and news about literature events in Essex. Some years ago, a decision was taken to design *Booktalk* in such a way that it would be accessible to the maximum number of readers, including those whose sight was failing. This magazine is a prime example of the maxim 'Good design is good for all'. All the text is either in large print or clear print. There is good use of contrast, colour and graphics, and thus it is accessible to large numbers of people who would struggle to read an ordinary newspaper as well as to people who have 20/20 vision. In addition, at least half of the titles covered in each issue are available in alternative formats. There is also now an audiotape called *Making a Choice* to assist with browsing.

Essex does not restrict its accessible design policy to print. It also runs a very successful and accessible browsing website entitled Ask Chris.[23] The site is interactive and readers can add their own book reviews and recommendations. You can choose the 'What Shall I Read Next?' feature and browse a wide range of titles with blurbs and reviews. If you wish, you can limit your search to large print or audio titles. All the pages are clear and easy to read with good contrast, good spacing and good-sized print even before magnification software is applied.

Almost everything about Essex libraries' reading promotion activities is geared to including visually impaired people, but not by segregating them. Even the book festival tries to include authors whose books are available in alternative formats, although with new authors this is not always possible. Although the book festival programme cannot yet be produced in clear print, alternative format versions are available. It was a bold decision to make the design of the magazine inclusive, but it has proved very successful and is a concept that could well have been adopted by other authorities. Sadly, it has not been taken up as widely as might have been hoped.[24]

Example 2: Bee Aware

As already mentioned, the two main problems for visually impaired readers are accessing material in the relevant format and browsing. The Essex examples above are very much in the browsing area, but for people who really are unable to engage with print at all, accessing material is also very difficult. There is a seriously limited amount of reading material in alternative formats (less than 5% of the annual UK publishing output) and, traditionally, public libraries have been unwilling to inter-lend alternative format stock. The Bee Aware scheme is intended to improve levels of interlending of material for visually impaired people.

> The Bee Aware Scheme is a national initiative to promote the inter library loan of alternative format material on behalf of visually impaired and print disabled people. The scheme was originally piloted within the North West, before being widened into a national scheme with the aid of Government funding in 1999.[25]

The scheme is available free of charge to all library authorities in England and works in conjunction with the RNIB National Library and the Calibre Audio Library. Details of how the system works and how to join the scheme can be obtained from the website. Libraries North West are anxious to extend the scheme as far and wide as possible and will send details to any authority which declines to inter-lend an item for a visually impaired person.

Again, uptake of this scheme has been patchy. There are areas of the country where there is almost blanket coverage and others where the Bee Aware scheme is barely encountered. The distribution pattern of use is not wholly geographical. While there is, in general, good coverage in the north of England, many southern authorities also use the scheme. But there are pockets in both north and south where authorities have not taken up the scheme, perhaps through ignorance, indifference or unwillingness to share their resources. In general, those authorities that have good services for visually impaired people tend to use the scheme, while those with poorer services do not.

Example 3: The Revealweb project (now incorporated into the RNIB National Library Service catalogue and into Unity UK)

Another attempt to address the problem of finding material in the relevant format is Revealweb, a database of accessible resources:

> On Revealweb you will be able to find out about:
>
> - a range of resources that are available in Braille, Moon, audio and digital talking books, large print and more by searching the *Catalogue of Resources*
> - contact details of organisations that hold titles in accessible formats and the terms under which they will supply them
> - who produces, loans or sells accessible material by searching the *Register of Suppliers*
>
> If you find the item you want contact the organisation directly as Revealweb cannot get hold of resources on behalf of users.[26]

This quote from the original Revealweb website (now defunct) succinctly sums up what the database was about. Searches could be limited by the format required, and the register of suppliers tells you how to get hold of items. Since the amalgamation of the NLB and the RNIB Library services, the separate Revealweb database, which was a groundbreaking venture, has been abandoned in favour of integrating the data into mainstream services such as the RNIB National Library Service catalogue[26] and the UnityUK[27] interlibrary loans service.

Many UK libraries have access to UnityUK and that will be their first port of call when looking to source a particular book in an alternative format. However, for those without access to UnityUK, the RNIB catalogue can be accessed online by sighted and visually impaired people.

Example 4: whichbook

Returning to browsing, there is whichbook:

> Instead of starting from the overwhelming choice of books available, whichbook starts from the reader and enables each individual to build the elements of that elusive 'good read' we are all looking for but do not quite know how to define.[28]

Whichbook concentrates on contemporary books, and allows readers a way into the great mass of books available each year. It allows you to customize the screen to suit you and gives instructions on how to do so. It works with screen readers. When searching for books, you can opt to select by large print, audio and/or other parameters. Clear concise instructions are given about how to use the site and you can link through to your local library authority to see if the books you choose are available for loan. If your authority has an interactive OPAC, you can even reserve your book online.

Whichbook is the brainchild of, and is managed by, the reader development agency Opening the Book and funded by the Big Lottery Fund. It is well used and popular among sighted people but sadly underused by the visually impaired community. This is largely due to a lack of understanding of its potential for visually impaired readers among frontline library staff.

Example 5: *A Touch Of . . .*

All the initiatives described above have continued. This last project is an example of good practice which had a big impact at its outset, and had the potential to be taken up and developed and still be ongoing, but which has largely faded from view. Again it addressed the browsing difficulties faced by visually impaired people, and offered libraries a way of enhancing their services.

A Touch Of . . . ran during 2000 to 2001 and was funded by the DCMS Wolfson Reader Development Fund. It was a partnership between the then National Library for the Blind, the RNIB, the then Calibre Cassette Library, the Society of Chief Librarians' reader development project Branching Out and Opening the Book. Much of the inspiration and work came from Opening the Book. It was the first national reader development project to reach visually impaired readers through an integrated approach involving specialist providers and the public library network.

New resources were created for visually impaired readers to enable them to try out a range of reading experiences before deciding which authors to try. Ten themed samplers were created, each containing reviews of and substantial excerpts from each of ten books, all available in alternative formats. Each sampler was intended to convey a feeling, such as *A Touch of Tension, A Velvet Touch* or *A Touch of Mischief*. Each English library authority was given a set of ten samplers in Braille, audiotape and CD formats, and offered training in how to use them.

Many authorities took advantage of the training and used the samplers well. Reading groups for visually impaired people were set up, using the samplers to choose books. In some cases authorities used the samplers to run events for visually impaired people in branch after branch over several years. Sighted reading groups liked the idea of the samplers so much that they borrowed the lists of titles for their reading lists. Some authorities built on the lists and extended the project in their own way, making it their own. However, these were the very few. In many authorities the boxes of samplers were never unpacked or, if they were, they went onto a shelf in a back room and never came off again.

Voluntary agencies like the NLB, the RNIB and Calibre cannot realistically be in the business of providing materials for public libraries. They can provide ideas, training, and examples of the sort of material which can be produced. However, it is then the job of the public library to take the idea and run with it. Sadly, that failed to happen except in a very few cases.

Conclusion

This chapter has provided a necessarily brief outline of the state of library services for visually impaired people and others who are isolated from literature in England today. It has covered the issues surrounding the provision of accessible services and bringing literature to visually impaired people. The need for staff training has been emphasized, as has the need to broaden libraries' views of the services needed by visually impaired people. In addition, some examples of best practice have been described, which show what can be done if the will (and the money) are there. Sadly, obtaining good library services for visually impaired people in England is a 'postcode lottery' and will remain so until there is greater understanding of the issues and the will to take the necessary actions at all levels of library management and service. In the last analysis we all have to remember that the reading needs of visually impaired and other excluded readers are no different from those of the public at large. It may also be salutary to note that a large cohort of post-war baby boomers are now entering retirement, and likely to be experiencing gradual loss of their sight: they are unlikely to accept curtailment of their reading as quietly as earlier generations have done.

Bibliography

1 DCMS (1999) Libraries for All: social inclusion in public libraries, [accessed 17 April 2007].

2 This list was taken from a CILIP Diversity Group web page which was available in October 2006 but which is no longer on the site. Current pages (as of April 2007) can be found at www.cilip.org.uk/specialinterestgroups/bysubject/diversity.

3 Braille Authority UK, www.bauk.org.uk [accessed 3 May 2007].

4 Moon Information Base [online] [cited 3/5/07], www.moonliteracy.org.uk/index.htm.

5 In this context the word 'interpreter' is taken to mean the person reading for the recording while the word 'reader' represents the ultimate customer.

6 Welsh, Irvine (1993) *Trainspotting*, Secker & Warburg.

7 Ellis, Bret Easton (1998) *American Psycho*, Picador.

8 Office of Public Sector Information, Disability Discrimination Acts 1995 and 2005, www.opsi.gov.uk/acts/acts1995/ukpga_19950050_en_1; www.opsi.gov.uk/Acts/acts2005/ukpga_20050013_en_1 [accessed 3 May 2007].

9 RNIB, Statistics: numbers of people with sight problems by age group in the UK, www.rnib.org.uk/xpedio/groups/public/documents/PublicWebsite/public_researchstats.hcsp [accessed 20 April 2007].

10 RNIB, About sight loss: changing the way we think about blindness, www.rnib.org.uk/xpedio/groups/public/documents/PublicWebsite/ public_rnib003680.hcsp#P19_1315 [accessed 20 April 20007].

11 RNIB, Statistics: numbers of people with sight problems by age group in the UK, www.rnib.org.uk/xpedio/groups/public/documents/PublicWebsite/ public_researchstats.hcsp [accessed 20 April 2007].

12 Ibid.

13 Ibid.

14 RNIB, About sight loss: changing the way we think about blindness, www.rnib.org.uk/xpedio/groups/public/documents/PublicWebsite/ public_rnib003680.hcsp#P19_1315 [accessed 20 April 2007]

15 Ibid.

16 Office of Public Sector Information, Disability Discrimination Acts 1995 and 2005' www.opsi.gov.uk/acts/acts1995/ukpga_19950050_en_1; www.opsi.gov.uk/Acts/acts2005/ukpga_20050013_en_1 [accessed 3 May 2007].

17 Calibre Audio Library, www.calibre.org.uk/ [accessed 4 May 2007].

18 RNIB, http://onlineshop.rnib.org.uk [accessed 4 May 2007].

19 RNIB, http://onlineshop.rnib.org.uk [accessed 4 May 2007].

20 RNIB, http://onlineshop.rnib.org.uk [accessed 4 May 2007].

21 RNIB, http://onlineshop.rnib.org.uk [accessed 4 May 2007].

22 BBC, Ongar Book Talk Group, www.bbc.co.uk/essex/content/articles/2007/02/28/ongar_booktalk_ group_feature.shtml [accessed 24 April 2007].

23 Essex County Council, Ask Chris, www.essexcc.gov.uk/applications/ask/default.htm [accessed 24 April 2007].

24 Information received by e-mail from June Turner at Essex Libraries.

25 North West Libraries Interlending Partnership: Bee Aware Scheme, www.lancashire.gov.uk/NWLInterlending/resources/beeaware/faqs.asp [accessed 24 April 2007]

26 Revealweb, www.revealweb.org.uk [accessed 24 April 2007]

27 UnityUK, www.combinedregions.com/about_unityuk/ [accessed 24 April 2007]

28 whichbook, www.whichbook.net [accessed 24 April 2007].

Chapter 4

Managing fiction: managing readers and writers

ANNE SHERMAN

Editors' preface

This chapter follows and develops the ideas introduced in earlier chapters by Jane Matthieson and Linda Corrigan. Anne Sherman considers how, over time, reader development has changed from being seen as an optional extra to being a central part of a public library's remit. In an often amusing way, Anne articulates the changing attitudes of staff to reader development activities and describes some of the schemes introduced.

Introduction

This chapter endeavours to show one public library service's changing perspective on reading development - no longer seen as an add-on or optional extra, but as an integral part of service delivery to bring literature to its readers. No criticism of staff or policy is intended, and the views expressed are those of the writer and not intended to be representative of the service as a whole.

Issues with book issues
Every person his or her book

A newspaper review of a newly published book was brought into a library and a request made for the item. The details were duly noted and appropriate forms filled in, the borrower appreciating that the book was not in stock but that his request would be passed on for the stock specialist's attention.

The title in question was *The Collector's Edition of the Lost Erotic Novels* by Anaïs Nin, and the *Guardian* review that had attracted the reader's attention raised a few weary eyebrows in the staffroom later in the day:

> [T]his self-styled Collector's Edition of erotica is indeed designed for those with specialist interests. There will, however, be just as many enthusiasts of the one-handed read as earnest bibliophiles squinting over their order forms. This is fascinatingly filthy stuff . . . After 600 pages of orifices, whips and feverish flutterings, the sordid depths of the human psyche will never seem quite the same again.[1]

The review was itself slightly feverish in tone, but the overall verdict was that this was a *recherché* and valid collection of erotica with contributions from masters of the art, and a timely reminder of the tenet 'Every person his or her book'.

The incident gave rise to a minor professional debate on what erotic literature was available or should be available through the library service, particularly as this genre does have a tendency to go AWOL. A selection of stock known unofficially as 'Bedroom Delights' is currently housed at Bibliographic Services, with books available for loan through the catalogue but deemed unsuitable for display in branches. However, these titles are not actively promoted to readers in any way, and their appeal may well have diminished with the advent of the internet. There are excellent reasons why books containing disturbing material should not be on the shelves; no one would want to come across the *ABC of Child Abuse*, edited by Roy Meadow. Although the *Association for Child Psychology and Psychiatry Review and Newsletter* recommends that it 'should be in the libraries of all who work with children at risk of abuse or neglect' the disturbing images make this book unsuitable for public display.

If libraries still recognize Ranganathan's second law of library science – every book has its reader – how far should the library service go to hold that book and to bring it and its reader together? In an environment dominated by numbers of book issues, promotion of stock is crucial, but are readers and writers being left out of the equation? Are libraries too book-centred and issue-led to promote literature to their readers effectively? This county's stock selection criteria states:

Stock selection supports the statutory responsibility to provide a service which is both comprehensive and efficient. In terms of stock 'comprehensive' is seen as the widest range of materials and titles appropriate to the various educational, informational, cultural and recreational needs of library users taking into account the Library Standards and any budgetary constraints.

The main focus for purchasing will be the likely popularity of a title, but having stock available to satisfy more obscure interests is also important.

The selection process will take into consideration the varied and specific needs of the communities within Cheshire.[2]

If the main focus for purchasing is the likely popularity of a title – that is, the likely number of issues – selection is informed by knowledge of the current readership only. Issues cannot increase significantly, and at best will remain stagnant, unless existing readers are challenged and encouraged to expand their choices, and new readers are drawn into using the library service.

Competition from supermarkets?

Our issues are down because of supermarket sales.

(Stock specialist)

In one week in 2007 Sainsbury's were offering titles by James Herbert, Jeffrey Deaver, Martina Cole, Nora Roberts, Jilly Cooper, Jodi Picoult, Maggie O'Farrell, Stuart Howarth, Fiona Walker and Richard Dawkins. Are libraries losing issues to these £3.99 impulse-buy paperbacks?

All our 45 hardback copies of Richard Dawkins' *The God Delusion* were currently on loan, with reservations waiting. And our 49 copies of Jilly Cooper's *Wicked!* were also all on loan, with reservations waiting. Issues may well be lost through the relative lack of paperback copies of *Wicked!* in libraries, and through the inability of our computer software to identify and locate alternative formats, such as hardback rather than paperback, for borrowers' reservations. The choice of titles at Sainsbury's was limited, offering bestselling authors but a representative mix of genres. However, if *The God Delusion* (described on its back cover as 'a timely, impassioned and brilliantly argued polemic on atheism') is flying off the shelves and reaching a new audience, these readers may in time rediscover their library where improved customer service, eye-catching displays and 'Quick Pick' impulse 'buys' are also on offer, at no cost. At the same time, the obvious attraction of the one-stop supermarket shop for time-hungry consumers needs to be acknowledged.

Taking a reader-centred approach to increase issues

The organization Opening the Book advocates the following approach:

> Traditionally, literature promotion has always started with the book and the author. Library services were designed to accommodate and manage the product – the book. The advent of reader development, and the reader-centred approach, challenged all that.
>
> In literature promotion, being reader-centred means starting with the reader and the experience of reading – giving them an insight into the experience awaiting them within the pages of the book. In libraries, the reader-centred approach offers a level of customer care which can inform and reinvent services across the board.[3]

I believe, with some reservations, that Opening the Book offers techniques for libraries to improve services, and at this moment in time that still means higher issues. Although Opening the Book has championed reader-centred activities such as reading groups, readers' days and improved stock, layout and IT resources, the object is to empower readers – to borrow more books. Happily, this comes without cost to the reader.

Reader development in Cheshire
Reading groups

> Reading groups – they're just a fad, aren't they? (Senior manager)

Reading groups are key to reader development, and to promotion of stock. Readers value peer reviews from members of their group with a shared reading history. Cheshire offers a Reading Group Collection, set up to encourage members of reading groups to expand their reading choices, to try something different and to discover new authors and new genres.

There is capacity for approximately 75 groups. The service is hugely popular and over-subscribed.

Staff involvement with reading groups has increased dramatically over the past year or so. A few years ago the unofficial policy was 'If we keep our heads down they'll go away', but the current provision is much improved. In January 2006 only eight out of 75 reading groups had staff involvement, whereas in summer 2007 there were 22 groups hosted in libraries with staff involvement, and the readership profile was far more varied with sixth-form college groups, teenager and family groups, and prison groups.

The 'reader recommends' model is used by some new groups, whereby books on a theme are read and shared, rather than one set title. This is more flexible for staff and readers, and truly reader-centred in that every member of the group can contribute new ideas and experiences.

> We don't have enough chairs for a reading group meeting.
>
> (Group librarian)

The former reluctance to encourage reading groups was always surprising; if a member of the public came into a library asking to borrow a book every month, with scope for additional loans, and expressed both an interest in attending literature-associated events in the future and a willingness to get involved with the library on a regular basis, why weren't they welcomed with open arms? Fortunately some were, and now library engagement with the public is increasing steadily. Recent reader events hosted by long-running library reading groups have raised their profile within the library service, contributing to the increase in new staff-run groups.

The comfort zone is still the core users, overwhelmingly white, female and aged 45–65, but a small number of socially inclusive initiatives arising from local demand – an English group for speakers of other languages (ESOL) and a lesbian, gay, bisexual and transgender (LGBT) group – are up and running and following on from the launch of 'Books on Prescriptions' (a scheme where GPs and health professionals work with library professionals to recommend to patients appropriate self-help books), further bibliotheraphy opportunities are being considered.

It has taken time but we're getting there. Reader development is genuinely embedded within the service. Opening the Book's 'Frontline' training course is rolling out through the service, and the regional support of

'Time To Read' (see Chapter 2) has been enormously beneficial as a strategic framework, as a means of sharing best practice between authorities and as a means of raising the bar in the north west of England, when working with readers and writers.

Writers' groups

Everyone is out of the building except for those people upstairs.
(Library assistant)

This regrettable remark referred to a group of poets attending a poetry workshop in a library, unaccountably regarded by the member of staff as not quite *bona fide* library users. Fortunately, this is very much an exception to the prevailing attitude. Recognition for writers groups is now established and there is a desire to celebrate local writing and local authors. Two libraries currently host writing groups, regular poetry and writing workshop programmes are held in libraries, and literature initiatives such as the Cheshire Poet Laureate scheme and the Lines on the Map[4] online project offer encouragement and development opportunities for local writers.

Promotion and partnerships

What is to be promoted and achieved through partnerships: literature, the activity of reading for pleasure, cultural activities in the community or just the continued use of libraries? A recent promotion in Macclesfield was very successful: MacclesFeast. This was essentially an evening of poetry and readings hosted by Jo Bell, the 2007 Cheshire Poet Laureate. The readings were all on the theme of food, and accompanied by a delicious selection of local food and drink. Local musicians provided entertainment in the interval. The library effectively hosted a small-scale farmers' market with poetic embellishments. Food lovers soaked up some verse and found it not indigestible, while poetry fans had the chance to meet food suppliers at this celebration of local produce orchestrated by the library manager with the support of the district council, placing the library very much at the heart of its community. The feedback was impressive, with compliments aimed at the poetry and produce alike.

Marketing and audience development

The library service plan for 2006-2007 stipulated that all libraries should deliver a fixed number of events, with the number of events relating to the size of branch. This announcement came with little guidance for frontline staff as to the nature of the events, and no additional resources were made available. Slightly alarmed, a small group of librarians and library assistants came together to address this requirement with a view to sharing best practice and pooling resources. The Book Themed Events Group was born.

Cracking the Code

Planning went ahead for a series of events to cash in on the media hysteria building up to the film release of the *Da Vinci Code*. A librarian with a background in graphic design produced some posters and tickets, available online for branches to amend and download as required. A comprehensive booklist was produced for displays, and staff put together a series of quizzes, codes and puzzles. Three large events were planned, each with a speaker to give a short illustrated talk on Leonardo da Vinci, with special reference to paintings referred to in Dan Brown's book, and local cinemas agreed to donate tickets as a prize. Smaller branches were able to tailor the resources and create their own 'Cracking the Code' event, or simply to produce a book display, according to their needs.

The evenings were well attended with excellent feedback, and attracted teenagers as well as older readers, giving Dan Brown fans plenty of opportunity to air opinions about the *Da Vinci Code*, although a surprising number of people had not read the book. The quiz took the form of a trail around the library, so participants explored those parts of the library they may not usually reach, which was itself a reader development opportunity to show off the range of stock on offer – a surprisingly effective manoeuvre. What was interesting was how much the readers enjoyed the evening activity. Many enjoyed the slide show, despite not usually attending art history events. One revealing comment was: 'It can be a bit boring listening to writers talk. This is much more fun.' This comment was taken very much to heart, and reader and literature development activity since has aimed for a high level of participation and social interaction whenever possible.

Cracking the Code was considered a success and the group was sanctioned to continue for a trial period until March 2007 with a small budget and a lot of freedom. The group was reborn as the Marketing and Audience Development group (MADg), with the aims of raising the profile of the library service both within the council and in the community, improving communications within the service and sharing best practice and pooling resources to make best use of staff time and energy. The budget enabled frontline staff to come forward with their ideas for local initiatives and small projects. Briefing sessions were given at group librarian and senior library assistant meetings, and in addition to a newsletter for all staff a comprehensive *Audience Development Events Guideline and Checklist* manual was produced.

A report is being prepared on the impact of this trial period and the group continues now on an official footing, directed to prepare a strategy for partnerships and working within Cultural Services. Effective marketing of the libraries service is a key part of this year's service plan. Raising the profile of literature and how libraries in particular can play a part paves the way for successful partnership working.

Fully Booked

Fully Booked[5] was the first major reader development project run by Cheshire Libraries in partnership with Social Services, running from October 2000 to June 2001. Funding was received from the Department of Culture, Media and Sport and the Wolfson Public Libraries Challenge Fund. This paid for the project manager post and the resource packs compiled to sustain the work. The overall aim of the project was to promote reading and the sharing of the enjoyment of reading among older people, who may find it difficult to access library services.

During the project the project manager ran reading group sessions in 12 day centres and community support centres across Cheshire. Readings and poetry on different themes were used to prompt conversations and reminiscences among clients. The sessions lasted from 30 minutes to an hour, and involved between two to 12 people. People with a wide range of needs and abilities enjoyed attending, and benefited from participating in the sessions. It was noted that people with visual impairments particularly enjoyed the exposure to books, which they could no longer read for themselves. People with dementia also took part and responded well.

It was initially envisaged that these reading groups in day centres would be set up to run along the lines of a conventional reading group, and that interested people would get together to choose books to read and then come back and discuss their reading. Following initial visits to the day centres, it became clear that this original idea would have to be revised. A different approach was needed. There were introductory sessions in the centres, during which people were encouraged to talk about their own reading habits and interests. The physical and mental frailty of the people attending the centres, their eyesight problems, low powers of concentration and memory loss, affected the practical running of a reading group along conventional lines. Other factors included the wide variety of needs and abilities among clients and the difficulty of forming groups of regular members as attendance at the centres can vary.

After some background reading and research into other reading and reminiscence work with older people, a programme of six sessions was drawn up to run weekly or fortnightly in six centres. The activity had to interest both those who enjoyed reading and those who did not generally read for pleasure, and to meet the needs of visually impaired participants. Each session was based around a theme which everyone would be able to relate to in some way, and included selected poems and readings from books that would be entertaining to listen to and would prompt memories and personal responses. The themes were: childhood, schooldays, travel, funny poems, wartime and Christmas. During the sessions, extracts were read from books and poems and people were encouraged to talk about what they had heard and share the memories these evoked for them.

The sessions provided a mentally stimulating activity and generated new topics of conversation. They enabled people to get to know each other and helped the staff get to know their clients better as individuals. As a small group activity, the sessions gave people an opportunity to share their thoughts and views and be listened to. This in turn helped them develop communication skills, feel valued and have greater self-esteem and confidence. At the same time, the exposure to books and poems generated interest in books and poetry among those able to read, and brought great pleasure to people no longer able to read for themselves.

Clients said:

It was an activity to look forward to, something a bit different.

It helped me to enjoy something I've always liked.

Always been interested in books and poetry, but it was nice for someone else to read because my eyesight is poor.

I liked listening and sharing memories of the past.

Staff commented:

> ·Certain clients took part in this project that would not normally
> take part in other activities. Also, those clients are still talking about
> it.

> It has given the clients a feeling of self-worth because their
> points were listened to and included, however big or small they
> were.

> Positive feedback about how they enjoyed it, and their moods
> seemed lifted for the majority of the afternoon, often recalling back
> to the sessions. Some clients became more confident and vocal
> as the weeks progressed.

> For the hour, they became a close group. The sessions enabled
> clients to reminisce, talk about their youth, life experiences. Took
> photocopies of the poems etc to share with their friends, carers,
> relatives.

Fully Booked was a very successful project based on a simple idea, which
had a significant impact on those who took part.

This project, and the next to be described, received external funding, and
both depend on outreach working and staff commitment for continued
success – a problem in the current climate of ongoing service re-organization
and staffing shortages.

Animate

The Animate project[6] was an ambitious reading development, arts and web-
based project established through a cross-service partnership between
Cheshire Arts, Libraries, Education and Social Services, with external
funding from the Paul Hamlyn Foundation.

Over a period of two years Animate aimed to offer looked-after children
– that is, children in the care of the local authority – improved access to
library services through a programme of welcome visits, an offer of two free
books for every child, ordered through the library PCs, free half-term art
workshops and a web-based story featuring material reflecting the children's
own stories. The aims and objectives of the project met criteria for the

national strategies Framework for the Future, Every Child Matters, and MLA's Inspiring Learning for All.

Frontline staff received training to raise awareness of the issues faced by looked-after children, and were also provided with *The Animate Library Handbook* – a resource compiled following feedback from library staff and distributed to all participating libraries. The handbook contained background information about the project and guidelines for the delivery of introductory welcome visits. Visits were planned in 18 libraries in January 2006 followed by a week of creative art workshops in three libraries over the February half-term week in 2006.

The project was marketed to children, carers and libraries. Host libraries had team meetings to discuss the project and go through *The Animate Library Handbook*, the project team members attended foster carer meetings to promote Animate and personal invitations were send out to all children in the county, with complementary letters to their carers and residential centres where appropriate. Invitations comprised both a personal letter and specially designed invitation postcard which children could show to library staff in order to claim their two free books. The project received media attention through local papers and radio.

Three artists delivered music, writing and graphics workshops for Animate Arts Week, and an *Artists Handbook* was developed. Of the 400 children invited, 50 children attended workshops – a low percentage but in line with the predicted take-up and with participation levels in comparable schemes for looked-after children. Those who did attend thoroughly enjoyed the workshops and the artists all commented positively about the quality and quantity of work produced.

As the project developed, the web story launch turned into a more significant event than just inviting an audience to come and see a new website in action. Instead, the launch also involved live activity by the young people themselves. Written material was developed into a series of short scenes which were then performed by a professional actress. Material from songs developed during the Arts Week was performed by three of the children, supported by professional musicians. The launch event was held in the Executive Suite at Macclesfield Town FC, and attended by over 70 looked-after children and carers.

A presentation on Animate was given at the Library and Information Show 2006 and at the Time To Read regional seminar Working with Looked-After

Children, with a further opportunity to share good practice by participation in a seminar at the 2006 PLG (Public Libraries Group) conference.

Cheshire County Council continues to offer two free books to all looked-after children, and will continue to strengthen links with its four residential care homes. Designated members of library staff have received further support and will carry out outreach activities, while a Writer in Residence scheme is also in the planning stages. Looked-after children are involved in a reader development project during 2008's National Year of Reading.

Animate placed access, participation and ownership at its core; its overall vision is to make looked-after children in Cheshire aware that there are positive outcomes for them as individuals. Libraries and books have a great deal to offer these children and their carers, particularly in relation to understanding what has happened to them, gathering facts and information about their pasts and realizing what opportunities and life experiences could be theirs in the future.

Animate also met the aims of the national initiative Their Reading Futures by addressing children's reader development in libraries, providing skills for frontline library staff in supporting young (looked-after) readers and supporting managers of children's services in planning and advocating their reading services. Reader development work originally targeted the adult audience in the county but an increasing number of pilot projects have been aimed at families, children and young people.

Reader development for children and young people

Why can't we do something for ordinary children?
(Senior library assistant)

Actually, there's quite a lot going on to promote literature to 'ordinary' children. At three staff away-days held in 2005, staff were asked to identify areas for development. Working with children and young people came top of the list.

As part of the MADg project, and building on a Time To Read family readers day, a Family Festive Fun Day was held in December 2006, with a guest poet and storyteller, food and craft activities. Much of the organization was taken on by the junior reading group who organized a quiz, prizes, and book displays extremely efficiently, and the event was enjoyed by a family audience of 59.

A teenage author was invited to Northwich Library for adult and teenage sessions. The turnout of teenagers was disappointing, but a repeat event is planned to take place in a youth centre or similar location. It is hoped that there will be interest in a teenage writing group over the summer break.

Libraries have been provided with funds for musical instruments to support growing RhymeTime sessions, and newly formed family reading groups have welcomed a professional storyteller. Two libraries now support children's poetry competitions. Summer holiday poetry and literature events are planned to tie in with the ongoing Reading Challenge, and to work in partnership with two local football clubs. Cheshire libraries run two teenage reading groups, and three junior/family groups, with support for three sixth-form and staff college groups – a significant increase in provision during 2006. A war game project is in the planning stages, with links to local games shop and youth centre The Hub as well as lone parent organizations. A graphic novel stock promotion with tie-in writing workshops was planned for late 2008. The 2006 Cheshire Poet Laureate worked with the Youth Parliament to produce a commissioned piece, *Don't Vote For Me*, performed at the January Youth Parliament elections.

In addition, three libraries hosted the Rhubarb Theatre Company's production of *Ssh!* for the Rural Touring Network over October half-term 2006, attracting audiences of over 80 to this delightful tale of Librarian Lil who wistfully hankers after the romance and adventure she finds in books – not, as some feared, a reinforcement of the stereotype librarian but rather an affectionate *homage* and firm avowal of the power of reading to transform lives.

Live music in the library

> How does this fit into your reader development remit?
>> (Librarian at 'Mr Hudson and the Library' live music event)

This question was asked half-way through the wildly successful event 'Mr Hudson and the Library' at Sandbach Library, and in the excitement of the moment went unanswered but not unnoticed. Cheshire was offered the opportunity to host a gig as part of the award-winning *Get it Loud in Libraries* project set up by Lancaster Music Library,[7] an initiative to encourage hard-to-reach teenagers and adults back into libraries. The up-and-coming band had just been signed by Mercury records, and was embarking on a UK tour of libraries from Edinburgh to Newport. The music was described as eclectic, a cross-pollination of hip hop and reggae, with bass, steel pans, electric drums, percussion and piano. The choice of venue was fortuitous, with marvellous staff who were enthusiastic about live music and prepared to give up their day off to act as roadies, provide home-cooked chilli and source all the music industry hospitality requirements. Their energy and enthusiasm were infectious, as 140 tickets sold out within a week and it seemed like the whole town was coming into the library to find out what was going on. In terms of increased book issues the project was a complete failure, but as a means of engaging with the community, raising the profile of the library service and trying something new, it was an overwhelming success. This event attracted a very different audience, aged largely 20–45, with a sprinkling of teenagers from the two local high schools. A member of the audience came up at the end of the evening with a gleam in his eye: 'I want to thank you; this is the best thing that's ever happened to this town!' What higher praise could you ask for from your users? The local paper chose to reflect on the changing role of libraries in a lighthearted but positive way:

What next – pole dancing in the register office?

An R & B band have been booked to perform in Sandbach Library. Since reading this I have been trying to picture the look on my old librarian Miss Crawshaw's face if members of a modern beat combo of any species wheeled their instruments and sound equipment into her jealously guarded domain. Would she go for them with a rolled umbrella, or bombard them with volumes of the Encyclopaedia Britannica? The former I should imagine, because it would go right against the grain for Miss Crawshaw to deploy volumes from the reference section as offensive weapons. But she'd certainly see them off before they had the chance to contaminate the premises with the likes of Little Red Rooster or Smokestack Lightning . . . Our village librarian had firm ideas about the library's role in the community, and they did not include hosting gigs by R & B groups. A tall bony woman, Miss Cranshaw frowned on people speaking in the library, let alone singing. Coughing, wheezing, sneezing or audibly breaking wind could get you slung out. It's hard to envisage her entertaining any kind of musical ensemble, from string quartets to Irish harpists. One year, she even ordered some carol singers to move on. Of course, I'm fully aware that public libraries have changed out of all recognition since the days when I silently picked up my weekly fix of Enid Blyton. But I'd no idea that they now doubled as rock venues.[8]

If only Miss Cranshaw was available for comment.

Conclusion

The following is a letter from a library user:

Dear Sirs

Last week I attended an author's evening at Chester Library presented by Kate Long, and I write to congratulate you on organising such an enjoyable evening. For a cost of £3.00 I was entertained, received a glass of wine, and as an aspiring writer was inspired by Kate to try harder with my own efforts. Kate herself was funny, informative and approachable and gave freely of her advice. Thank you for organising this event. I have been a life long supporter of libraries (as an avid reader I can't afford not to be) and I have always encouraged my children to do likewise. I have never before attended an author's evening though, which on reflection is much to my loss. I do hope that you continue to programme these events as I would very much like the opportunity of attending more.

Thank you once again.

Yours faithfully, etc.[9]

It would appear that libraries are getting something right. And when they do get that something right the impact is evident. Reader-centred, book-centred or library-centred – partnerships and promotions ideally deliver a balance of mainstream activities to add value to people's engagement with literature, to encourage readers and writers to participate in the cultural opportunities offered, to attract new or lapsed users back and to improve the image of libraries as welcoming community spaces. With a shifting focus on participation and impact rather than footfall and issues, libraries will continue to play a crucial role in bringing literature to readers.

Bibliography

1   Briscoe, J. (2005) Porn by the Yard, *The Guardian* (31 December),
     http://books.guardian.co.uk/review/story/0,,1675023,00.html#article_
     continue.

2   Cheshire County Council Libraries (2006) *Information and Culture Staff
     Handbook* (November).

3   Van Riel, R.and Fowler, O., *Opening the Book*,
     www.openingthebook.com/otb/page.asp?idno=363.

4   www.cheshire.gov.uk/readersandwriters/writers/linesonthemap/home.htm.

5   www.cheshire.gov.uk/readersandwriters/readers/fullybooked/.

6   www.animatecheshire.co.uk/.

7   www.lancashire.gov.uk/libraries/events/lancastermusic/index.asp.

8   Cookman, A. (2007) 'What Next – pole dancing in the register officer?' *The
     Sentinel* (29 January), 8.

9   Letter to library service, 27 June 2006.

Chapter 5

Getting into reading

JANE DAVIS

Editors' preface

With the growing interest in reader development and the increasing sense
that libraries can have an important new role in social regeneration, this
chapter about a public library service's involvement in the Get Into Reading
project will make inspiring reading.

This chapter takes reader development from the practitioners, librarians
and partners directly to the reader. The voices of readers are important:
they have a lot to say to the information professional. This chapter shows how
readers pick up on staff attitudes, and illustrates some of their attitudes to
libraries.

Introduction: foul-weather friends

My mother was a docker's daughter who won a scholarship to a public
school. Her life went badly askew during her marriage and divorce, and she
died in unhappy circumstances in her early 50s. An avid reader of trashy
novels, she liked good books too, and during my younger childhood,
when things had not yet become too bad, she read to me: *Heidi*, *The Wind
in the Willows*, *Tales from the Arabian Nights*, *My Family and Other Animals*.
One of my strongest memories is of her pulling her hair down and over her
face to recite some of the witches' stuff from *Macbeth*: 'Where the
place?/Upon the heath/There to meet with Macbeth.'! She would get us all

screaming and hiding behind the couch. That was the residual benefit we got from her scholarship.

I grew up as the oldest of four children in a poor and pretty chaotic single-parent family. My local library, Toxteth in Liverpool, was a refuge. They let me take out adult books on a junior ticket. Aged 12 and recently graduated from *The Borrowers* and *The Hobbit*, I read *Strike the Father Dead*, a novel by John Wain. I don't think I understood it, but that didn't seem to matter. I read *Under Milk Wood* and borrowed an LP of it. However, I left school at 16 with just two GCEs – English language and art – two you could get without doing any work. English literature – which we called 'books' at home – was a mainstay against unhappiness but the way you had to 'do' it at school seemed unnatural and required a level of discipline and concentration I didn't have. Themes in *Romeo and Juliet*: what a weird way to talk to 15-year-olds! I truanted or just blanked out.

Then, as a young single mother, I was lucky enough to bump into 1974-style feminism, with its conscious-raising, study groups and book-swapping circles. It was here I learned to read with purpose. 'The personal is political' was a feminist slogan of those days, and the emphasis on reading for personal meaning excited me. I wasn't so keen on the books of political theory my friends offered, but the novels (*The Female Man* by Joanna Russ, *Orlando* by Virginia Woolf, *Woman on the Edge of Time* by Marge Piercy) and increasingly the poetry seemed to reach deep places in me.

I needed these books to help me shape a life for myself and I read hard, everything I could lay my hands on (by women), including the better-known classics (*Jane Eyre*, *Wuthering Heights*, *Persuasion*). Eventually in my early 20s I went to university to read English and met an inspiring teacher, Brian Nellist. He taught me how to escape the feminist straitjacket in which I'd tied myself – how to lend myself to a book or a point of view not my own so it became possible to read things with which I wasn't immediately *simpatico*. As Brian's student, I learned that reading a book is like meeting a person: those that seem difficult at first sight could turn out to be your best friends. An easy read is a fair-weather friend (which is why so many of us take them on holiday) but great books are your foul-weather friends. I was lucky to graduate from university having learned that.

Getting great books out of the university

I had been teaching English literature in the Continuing Education programme at Liverpool for 15 years, free to choose what and how I taught. I put on courses about things I hadn't read in order to get myself to read them: 17th-century lyric poetry, or *Paradise Lost* or *Clarissa*. I couldn't teach these things as an expert so I simply offered 'reading courses'. Over time this settled into a distinctive method. I would read aloud portions of whatever was on the menu, and then after a page or two we would go back over what we'd read trying to work out what was happening. At a Saturday day school, a group of ten to 20 willing adults from many walks of life would read something together, say Shakespeare's *Sonnets*. Over the day's four 90-minute sessions we might concentrate on perhaps as few as six poems, perhaps a total of 50 lines. We never talked 'about' the book; we simply tried to read it. My students joked that I was getting slower and slower and that soon we'd spend all day reading one line. But the courses were well attended. We all felt, I think, that we were getting something real out of it.

I was unhappy, though, that my classes, made up of people from many walks of life, didn't contain anyone like the girl I'd been at 20: uneducated, needy, poor and rough around the edges. People like that couldn't afford the fees for continuing education classes, and if they'd had the money they still wouldn't have thought of coming to the university – yet what we were doing in those classes, I thought, was something absolutely anyone could do. Not only that, anyone who did do it would get something from it.

I applied for a £500 grant and used the money to run a five-week project, called Get Into Reading (GIR), in two different centres in deprived areas of the Wirral. The idea was to recruit adult students enrolled at a community college to a weekly group in which people could learn to read for pleasure. I was looking for people who weren't readers. I wasn't sure if the 14 people who signed up for those two pilot groups *could* read. So I prepared myself to read aloud and took photocopies of a short story, *Schwartz*, by Russell Hoban, and some poems, chosen because they were relatively easy to read but also personal favourites. They included Tennyson's *Crossing the Bar*.

In retrospect *Schwartz* was an odd choice: it is not an easy read. It concerns a writer suffering from writer's block. He goes out to get away from himself and wanders into a story about blockages, Theophilus Monk, guilt, a stone lion and a chart of the Chinese alphabet. It is mildly weird and requires confidence on the reader's part. And yet in essence the story is simply this: a man faces himself, finds himself wanting, owns up to that and feels a bit better. I chose it because I thought we've all been there; everyone has had that middle-of-the-night moment.

The story takes about 20 minutes to read. F, an unemployed welder, interrupted to say, 'This guy's been on the wacky baccy', and that made everyone laugh. But later it was F who made a perceptive comment about how it easy it is to get stuck in life. And at the end of the session it was also F who said, 'So when are you bringing all the good stuff? Shakespeare? Tolstoy? The poshknobs have all the best stuff. Why can't we try it?'

I'd never have thought of reading Shakespeare with that group, but F's way of putting it reassured the less confident members and gave us a good context. We were just having a look at what it was 'the poshknobs' loved so much. The next week I brought *The Winter's Tale* with me.

In both groups, the poem *Crossing the Bar* made people cry:

> Sunset and evening star,
> And one clear call for me!
> And may there be no moaning of the bar,
> When I put out to sea,
>
> But such a tide as moving seems asleep,
> Too full for sound and foam,
> When that which drew from out the boundless deep
> Turns again home.
>
> Twilight and evening bell,
> And after that the dark!
> And may there be no sadness of farewell,
> When I embark;
>
> For tho' from out our bourne of Time and Place
> The flood may bear me far,
> I hope to see my Pilot face to face
> When I have crost the bar.[1]

In the first group, a young woman, T, cried silently as I very slowly read the poem aloud. I looked up and she was wiping tears away. She flapped a hand. 'It's okay – go on.'

I read the poem again, and everyone nodded, as if they had 'got' something, but we were all looking to T. 'It's my Dad,' she said. 'He died last year. It just seemed to . . . put it into words.'

In the other group it was the second or third week when I got around to the Tennyson. A newcomer, D, had just walked in, late, and settled herself. I started to read and had not got far into the poem, perhaps the second stanza, when she started to cry. There was real pain in her response. I said, 'Shall I stop?' but, like T, she nodded from behind her tissue and simply said, 'Go on.'

I went on. D continued to cry. I said, 'We'll read something else.'

'My daughter died six weeks ago,' said D. 'I can't help it. Go on, don't read something else. Just carry on.'

You could feel everyone in the group suffering, a mixture of social embarrassment (we were a very new group and didn't know each other very well) and real pain on behalf of D, and perhaps a bit of pity for me, too, as the person responsible for trying to sort the situation out. There was a sense of goodwill mixed with the pain. Everyone wanted it to be all right, not just to stop or to go away, but to be somehow *right*, to be okay. Yet here was this stranger with her very recent, painful bereavement. It was my job to bring about a solution and I didn't know how to do it. I started looking in my bag for the alternative choice of poem I'd brought with me.

'Go on, read it again,' D insisted, making powerful eye contact. This time as I read she cried, and she spoke about lines of poem, and others spoke too, about what the poem might mean, what it meant to us. When it was over, she folded the poem up and put it in her bag and thanked me. F, the welder, leaned over and covered her hand with his own. 'Well done, kidder,' he said. 'You were brave.'

I realized then that I had stumbled into something important - that getting literature out of the university, out of the classroom, was going to have real social consequences.

F died a year later from a sudden and very aggressive brain tumour. He continued to attend the group until a few weeks before the end. When one of the group visited him in hospital he was reading Tolstoy's *Death of Ivan Ilytch*.

Talking to readers

G

G is a full-time carer in his 70s. He attends 'The Book Break', a GIR group for carers.

J: **How long have you been involved in Get Into Reading?**

G: It's two years ago last February. I look after my wife you see, and once a month we go to the Stroke Group and one of the ladies was invited to spread the word and she came and had a chat. . . . She left a few leaflets, and one day when my wife was in respite, I was at a loss of what to do and I went down to the disabled place in Birkenhead and that was when a new leaf turned on the page, a new story started. Yes, a very enjoyable day, and it all started from there. I'd never done anything like reading since I left school, and I left school at 14 and that's 60 years ago now. Why go? Something to learn. You see I've been a carer, and had nine years taken out of my life, because apart from looking after my wife I didn't go out, except on once a month to this Stroke Group. Apart from that I just sat there and talked to her, and she's going through a phase where she doesn't want to talk now.

J: **Were you ever worried that you didn't have a background in reading? I mean did it ever make you think 'Oh I'm out of my depth' or . . .**

G: Well yes, to tell the truth I would say that. I probably am out of my depth, many a time I have been out of my depth, but the people that look after you, the group, they help you, encourage you. It doesn't really matter. And we find out for ourselves that if you want to be involved, you can be involved, but if you don't want to, if you just want to sit and listen, and read to yourself, you don't have to get involved. It's up to you. This has expanded me into reading poems, and listening to how other people read poems. I'm not a natural reader, but I am a natural listener and I was encouraged. . . . The reading in itself will get you out of your situation, indeed it does. It changes your mind and takes the problems away from you.

J: **Does it help being in a group with other carers?**

G: Yes, because what we do we come here, we ask how we are and we let go for a few moments and that's it, we don't carry on with our problems, we forget our problems when we read.

J: **Tell me about some of the things you've read**.

G: The thing which really sticks out is *An Inspector Calls*. I *was* the Inspector. Another one was *Hobson's Choice* . . . oh it's a good one, it's a good one. You see we're sort of reading it, and reading our parts on the hoof. And I enjoy it. You're looking at it from many points of view, you see different perspectives. We don't argue. We're sitting at this table, looking at the same book, but we're seeing it from different angles, different points of view. That's what it's like. I wasn't a literary person before. I liked reading . . .

J: **What kind of things would you have read before?**

G: History and that. What has happened . . . the world's exploits you might say . . . . I was a construction worker, did you know that? And they say things like 'manual worker' as if we are just hands, but you've got a brain. Indeed you have.

R

R is a GIR volunteer who worked with us for many months.

J: **How long have you been involved with GIR?**

R: Three years now. I was living at the YMCA and all of a sudden we found out there was a book group coming in. So I volunteered to go to it, and it just took off from there. Then you started pointing me towards Ridgeway [Ridgeway Library, with a very well established GIR group] and I ended up at Ridgeway. It was just such an interesting thing. I enjoyed doing it; I enjoyed helping the others to find it too.

J: **Had you ever done anything like this before?**

R: Nothing whatsoever. Well, I read privately, yes. I used to read to the wife, if she had a book and wanted a rest I would read to her and I used to enjoy it. And when I went to the groups and we were reading out loud, I enjoyed it. I was thinking about it yesterday; I loved *Jackanory* as a kid, watching it on the telly and the idea of somebody reading, or being read to, is splendid, I love it. It's comforting, it's reassuring, it's restful.

J: **What else do you get out of being in a GIR group?**

R: I enjoy the speaking to people, talking, the social interaction with everybody. I love it. I've made so many great friends.

J: **Do you think there are any health implications of GIR?**

R: Yes, definitely. It's a calming influence, it brings you down and it helps you to concentrate more instead of thinking about what's going wrong in your head; it makes you think about what you *can* do. It guides you to a focus. When you read you have to be focused. And when you're in the reading groups you have to be focused because you're reading things to other people, and that makes things easier. . . . You're on the spot.

   We've got people with mental problems, and they get kicked out of hospital after seven weeks and get told the community will take care of you. They've got care in the community, but they've got nowhere for them to go. But if they've got reading groups, they've got places where they can go and they can interact with other people; they can learn what living with other people is about.

J: **Can you talk about what you've been reading?**

R: With all my problems some of the books we've been reading have been very deep. I mean *Sons and Lovers*, that was a deep book, a book with mental issues, psychological issues, and that hurt in many ways, what with my marriage and everything. Mr and Mrs Morel, they were wrong for each other from the start. That reminded me of my marriage and that was very hard.

J: **So wouldn't people say, 'Don't read it then'?**

R: Yes but you have to read it, otherwise you're censoring yourself. *Sons and Lovers* is a book that's been going along for so long now. It's a book that you *want* to read. It's a book that is of interest because of who it comes from, Lawrence. It's a book of life, even if it's painful. I mean why do people write these books? Because they are painful and they come from their own experiences. It's got to be done because people have to learn, and we learn by reading books.

J: **But if you've got somebody who's already depressed, homeless people from the Ark Shelter or YMCA, really troubled, why give them such material?**

R: Yes but they picked up on *Of Mice and Men*, the lads at the YMCA, because they're people like them, people they understand. Say you were to give them Charlotte Brontë, it would be very difficult for them to understand. But you give them something that they understand to start with, and they'll build on that, and then they'll transfer over to other things. Now I love Shakespeare. I love Shakespeare, I really do. I mean sitting there taking on a role in a Shakespeare play, reading it out to a group, it's brilliant, it's absolutely brilliant. I love that. *Measure for Measure*. I mean because we've got the trip down to London, to the Globe. It's a highlight, brilliant.

J: **Some people would find it strange that you could identify with characters in Dickens or Shakespeare because they're from hundreds of years ago.**

R: Well if you've had a bad life, a bad life took place a hundred years ago as well as today. What they went through then, there are people going through today, sometimes even more. I mean there are still Fagin characters . . . there are drug dealers out there who use kids, preying on young kids. It's *Oliver Twist*. But don't forget that if you find out that someone else is going through what you've gone through, you don't feel quite as bad. You think, 'If they've been through this, and look what they've got out of it, if there's a happy ending at the end of this book, I could have a happy ending.'

J: **But in *Of Mice and Men* there isn't a happy ending. Why should guys in the YMCA enjoy that?**

R: With all of these men, they live such aggravated lives, in everything they do they're tensed up. Getting through that tension is something that reading can do for them because you stop them, you stop in their tracks, bump, that's it. It's worth it. But librarians – you can go into the library and not one of them will smile at you, not one of them. They think you're dirt. The lads from the YMCA – they don't make them welcome. They treat them like dirt. What they need is . . . they need to know how to deal with people.

M and B

M and B are members of a 'Feel Better With A Book' group set up especially for mental health service users. Many of the members have depression, and others have more severe conditions. The group meets weekly for two hours.

J: **How long have you been involved in your GIR group?**

M: From the start, about three years ago. I saw a notice in the library, 'If you're feeling down and you want to meet friends', something like that. I thought that's for me, because I'd had a breakdown and I was re-starting my life in a new place and I needed to meet people. At the same time I get a lot out of it. The books I read here, I wouldn't read on my own.

J: **A lot of people wouldn't want to read some of the books that we read. Have you found it upsetting?**

M: Maybe at the beginning I might have found it a bit sad but I think it's good because when you have been through something you need to talk these things out. It's part of your life; it's good to talk about it. The kind of books we read here, we talk about and take into our lives; it's not just spouting out ideas, we really think about it. One of the first books was *Jane Eyre*. I wanted to do the classics because I had wasted the chance at school. I had other things on my mind.

J: **Would you have ever gone to a literature course or class?**

M: No. At that stage all I wanted was company. At the beginning I just used to sit and listen; sometimes I couldn't get my ideas together. You're not obliged to say anything. You can just sit and listen and partake; that's what I found was good. You don't want to feel forced to do things. But in the reading group I realized that nothing was expected of me so I started to relax and that's when you start joining in. And with some of the other people in the group, who couldn't say anything . . . no one has bothered them, and they keep coming back. We're there to support each other as well.

J: **Critics might say, 'Why can't she go to a support group for people with depression?'**

M: No. It's not the same. There I would feel that terrible pressure. I don't want to be talking about what's wrong with me all the time, bringing it up. This is a different way: it's support but at the same I'm meeting new people and reading new stories – because I do like reading. I find support groups a bit invasive. For me this has been a therapy, definitely. And it was something that was missing from mental health therapy; they didn't have anything like that.

J: **Did you read before?**

M: The situation that I was in, we didn't have a chance to read. I was in a convent for 38 years. They did have some classics and things – some Dickens – but we weren't encouraged to read; it was only religious reading.

J: **Has GIR affected your confidence?**

M: Oh yes, confidence – being able to speak in a group – I didn't have that before. I'd had a lot of responsibility. We looked after elderly people; I had staff under me. I had wanted to come out of the order for a long, long time. And when I did come out, it was so hard. I had to start all over again, rebuild my confidence. When I was in hospital, I met a gentleman who had had a very bad time, who didn't think he could get out. He said, 'There's nothing for me out there,' and I thought, 'Oh God, that's going to be exactly the same for me.' He said, 'There's absolutely nothing.' When you're coming out and you're trying to get on your feet, it seems that there is nothing for people.

I started going to the library to do an ECDL [a European Computer Driving Licence] because I wanted to learn about computers. But sometimes I just sat at the computer and cried. Then I thought, I need something in the week and I saw this and thought, 'Well that can be my Friday.' And little by little it built up. That was a really gentle way of getting to meet people.

J: **Is there anything you've read in your group that has really moved you or touched you?**

M: *Of Mice and Men* moved me; it's very sad. But you see, when you've been through something like we've been through, you've got more empathy for stories like that. I like the one we're reading now, *Adam Bede*. I read and think, 'Oh I love it!' What I like about it is that we can always find something to talk about in these books. Now I have a book of poems, and I am able to look at it and understand it a bit. Before, that would have done my head in!

B is a member of the same group. She has had severe mental health problems for many years.

J: **How long have you been involved in GIR?**

B: About a year and a half. I first went because I had a mental health problem and I wasn't getting out much and this was a way of getting out. At first I couldn't even follow the reading, I just listened, but as time went on I got interested, really got involved, not just in the reading – they're such a nice crowd and made me feel so welcome – I really, really enjoy it now. I've got to be honest, I have never been a good reader; I could never concentrate properly because of my mental health problem. Even in school, people used to say, 'Oh have you read such and such?' and I could just never get into it. But I really enjoy reading now and my daughter and granddaughter are made up with me because they do a lot of reading and they're quite surprised to see me sitting down with a book! They're pleased for me and I'm pleased myself.

J: **If you weren't a keen reader how did you come to go to the group?**

B: I think I'd seen it advertised. I can tell other people it's a good thing to do, even if you're not a reader, to come along. You'd be surprised how you get involved with the books. The story might be a bit slow, or not to my taste, but we keep with it, with the group. You've got to consider the rest of the group because they might really like this book. You've got to give and take. . . . I'm glad I did it this way because it's got me into trying to consider other books which I might not have got into. I've got books lined up now because people have bought me them as presents. . . . I've ended up taking an interest in reading.

Libraries have always put me off. I just haven't got an idea at all where to go in a library. I know you can get the help off the librarian, but my confidence has only built up over the years. . . . I wouldn't go. I'd be lucky to even read the paper when I'm really unwell. I'd just watch the news or listen to it on the radio.

J: **Has Get Into Reading affected your confidence?**

B: Well my confidence has been building a lot anyway. I go to a women's group in the drop-in centre, and the teacher wasn't coming in, so the other week, I said to the group – there was only about five of us – 'Would you like to come next week and we'll discuss something?' I'd got this new book about healthy eating, so I took it. I wasn't nervous or anything because I knew we all had mental health problems, so I knew they wouldn't be expecting something marvellous. So I took the book . . .

J: **You're spreading it! Tell me some of the books you've read in the group . . .**

B: We're reading *Adam Bede* at the moment and it's starting to get a bit more exciting now, so that's one, and *Jane Eyre*. Plays. And we've been to see plays at the theatre. That's another nice thing about the group - the plays. Most people wouldn't think of going, thinking it's posh, but it gives them an insight into what they can go to see . . . very different things. I think it's good for people to go to see things like that . . .

J: **Does reading aloud make a difference?**

B: Yes it does - instead of taking the book away - well there are groups like that. . . . That wouldn't appeal to me. I wouldn't go, I don't think. But, I'm not saying I wouldn't do it now because I'm a bit more into it. At first I wouldn't have done that. I'd have felt very intimidated by the other readers.

J: **But not now?**

B: Not now.

V and C

V and C are two readers from the Ark homeless shelter. They have both been through very difficult times in recent years.

J: **How long have you been involved with the reading group?**

C: Well I've been there since September last year and we still go don't we? To me that says it all.

V: And we get on as a team, don't we? And as friends, don't we?

C: Yes. Sue's [GIR project worker] got into a habit of doing plays - I was in a pantomime years ago; it brings back a few memories. And it's good listening to V and the others who read.

J: Did you feel shy about reading out loud?

V: Well I was at first, but not now. I was really shy wasn't I?

C: At first yes. But when V first moved into the Ark, I was one of the first men to come and talk to her. I got some backchat off the lads but that's water off a duck's back to me.

It is good to make friends. There's always one you can talk to at least. And I hope V . . . I can talk to V . . .

J: Did the reading group help with that?

V: Yes. It gave me more confidence. I'm reading books for my grandchildren now and can put smiles on their faces.

J: Before you came to the reading group how much did you read?

V: Not a lot, nothing.

C: I used to read when I was on my own a few years ago - war books and that. I'm getting back into reading now . . . and I can read more, especially when I'm on my own.

J: Do you think your concentration has improved?

C: I've always had that but it just . . . it just relaxes you and you can think more then; when you're involved in a book, it makes you think more.

V: When I was at home I could read certain things but I wasn't really bothered. But since I've been involved . . .

J: Tell me about some of the books you've read.

C: *Mice and, Mice and . . .*

V: *Of Mice and Men.* It was fantastic.

J: But did you find it sad?

V: Yeah I did, didn't you?

C: Yes I did.

J: But doesn't that matter?

V: No. It makes you think . . .

C: It makes you realize . . .

V: About what the person's feeling, everything like that? And we talk about what we've done all week - things like that.

C: It's even . . . I'm not too sure if V's got books off Sue. Some of the lads have, and I've got a couple of books in my house.

J: **So you borrow books from Sue as well?**
V: Yes, to read by myself.

J: **Would you ever go to the library?**
V: No. It's just not my style, my way of life. No.
C: You know, to me going to the library is something that is a long way off . . .
V: Yeah, it's a long way off isn't it?

J: **Okay, tell me about another book you've read**.
V: What was it, *Kes*? That was good.
C: *Kes*, yeah. It's two brothers, and one out of spite kills the bird. So it's . . . It's good for me especially because I've had personal . . . because I've had things happen similar to that . . . not exactly the same but . . .
V: It's like a picture. You can picture it.

J: **Somebody might say, 'Oh that's another sad book . . .'**
V: Well the first time I started it seemed to be about sad stories and I could have done without that, but I have come back to the group haven't I? When we read, don't we, we've always got a smile on our faces. We get to know each other, learn more.
C: Yes. Even though I know V, you know a person differently in the group because you are listening, talking. It is quite daunting – even though there's only four or five of us there, it's quite daunting.

J: **Because it's vulnerable, do you mean?**
C: Yes. When you get deep into it, and when people open up a bit more, like V has, and I've seen a lot of changes in V, a lot of changes. I feel that the five of us, even Sue was apprehensive at first, but somehow the group has . . .
V: We help each other with words. We've all had troubles.

J: **Why do you think reading aloud is important?**
C: Because you get engrossed in the first two episodes, and then you won't

put it down. Once you're over the hurdle, as some say.

V: Sue does the reading first, and then if people want to carry on they can.

C: Sue gives you the opportunity if you want to. She doesn't pressurize or nothing like that. She'll ask you if you'd like to read a few lines. But it is a big step.

V: It is to me. Yes, yes. I've read. It's a friendly surrounding.

J: **Tell me, why is it valuable?**

V: Well, so we can get to sit as we're doing and read books and get to see our smiling faces.

C: Yeah, but it's also got to be the right situation.

J: **So if we said this is available in the college or the library, come if you want . . .?**

C: No, we'd want to walk right past there . . .

V: No, I'd never . . .

C: I've moved on from the Ark now and I still go there for the reading group and people say you must love it there, but it's not that. It is – we're still learning, I'm learning, even though I'm in a difficult situation. Why not be in a good environment and just sitting down and reading? I've sat on the bus many a time and looked at people reading and thought, 'How boring is that.' But now I'd think twice about that and I'd say, 'Hang on, he must be engrossed in that book.' It gets you involved, and now I understand why people put their marker in the book. . . . I was just thinking then, you're writing a book, or an article or that; imagine me in a book!

J: **When I write this up I'll get Sue to bring it along so you can see it.**

C: It's a pleasure. Thanks.

J: **No, it's _my_ pleasure. Thank _you_.**

Some library staff speak

Julie Barkway, a senior librarian with Wirral Libraries, has been seconded to GIR for a year with money from the Esmee Fairbairn Foundation, and has helped Jill Ashton, a library assistant from Heswall library, set up a GIR group at a social services centre for adults with learning disabilities. The day centre is a five-minute walk across the road from the library. The group meets weekly for an hour or more. The day I attended there were 18 people there. None of them can read. Jill read from *Charlie and the Chocolate Factory*, and Julie read William Blake's poem, *The Tyger*.

J: **Can you say how being involved in GIR has affected you?**

Julie: From a professional point of view, the thing that I've noticed is that it's dealing with a completely different client group. The people who come to our GIR groups are noticeably different people than use our libraries for other things. It's a group of people who just would never cross the door. We've got people with different kinds of health problems . . . we've got people with dyslexia . . . there are people who can't read because they're on medication, or under too much stress, and they can just have something read to them. They can participate if they want, but they don't have to participate if they don't feel like it.

Jill: As a library assistant, it's brought to me a completely different aspect of the job because I was getting very fed up with the day-to-day library stuff, so to go out and to do this, the outreach work, is absolutely fantastic. I enjoy it that much; it is the highlight of my week.

J: **Tell me what you do.**

Jill: We go out to the group and there's about 15 or 16 adult learners, with Down's syndrome and with severe mental and physical difficulties. We are reading *Charlie and the Chocolate Factory* at the moment. I read and we have some interaction and chatter. People in the group bring a lot of discussion into it, probably discussion that they don't have normally . . . things go off on a tangent. With *Charlie* we talk about our favourite chocolates . . .

Julie: It can start off with something quite light and then people can start talking about what's going on in their own lives without feeling on the spot. People talk and express themselves.

J: **Tell me about how you'd choose the books. Is there a wide range of ability in the group?**

Jill: There are extremes, but there are also people who are similar, so it is quite hard to judge. I just go on personal choice. I went through books that really stuck in my mind. So it's come from my enjoyment really, and the books that I have enjoyed as a child and as an adult.

Julie: And it's startling how the group can concentrate for a whole hour. I don't think the staff believed that people at that centre could concentrate for that long.

Jill: No, because at first they were worried, weren't they, that it was going to be too long?

Julie: But everyone's enjoying it. It's amazing because the people at this day centre are severely disabled and I think the staff were a bit sceptical as to how it would go at first. But now they really embrace it.

Jill: But I don't think other library staff have much idea what we do. Lots of people within the service would think, 'Well, that's a good thing but you wouldn't get me doing it.'

Julie: You do have to have certain qualities and if you don't have those qualities it wouldn't . . .

J: **What do you think they are?**

Jill: It's approachability, isn't it? You've got to be comfortable with other people. It's confidence as well; you have to be prepared to take risks.

Julie: And not feel bad because things don't work straight away. And you do have to have empathy with people who are more vulnerable. Not everybody has that.

Jill: Some people can't see people with problems as human; they just see the problem.

Julie: It's got to change, and I think there's an awareness that it's got to change and it will change at some point in the future and then we will be looking at a different kind of person being recruited for library work . . .

Jill: I could do it all day, every day. I could go to a different centre all day and just not get fed up of it at all because each group is different and all the people have got their own individual characters, and so therefore what you get out of one session you won't get in another place and vice versa.

J: **Did you feel nervous, when you went to the day centre for the first time?**

Jill: At first, apprehensive because I didn't know what to expect, but the minute I got in there I felt like it just sort of came naturally really. . . . Julie was doing *Charlie and the Chocolate Factory* in another day centre so we had that, but I took some silly poems that I had about chocolate and some other bits and bobs like, silly picture books and so on, so I came quite prepared and as you go on that's what you realize. You think about what you're going to take each week.

J: **Advice to somebody setting up a group would be . . .**

Julie: Just not to worry, keep on going, it takes time. People who are coming are vulnerable so it's a slow build-up.

Jill: Just get out there and try something!

Conclusion

When I started the Get Into Reading project I had no idea what would develop. All I knew was that I wanted to extend the reach of the books I loved, books which had sustained and helped me personally. The growth of the project has been largely to do with its success in meeting an almost invisible need. Few people are conscious of a need to share conversations about the stuff contained in great books, but that doesn't mean the need is not there. As one of our first beneficiaries said to me, 'You need it, but you don't know you need it.' We are more aware of our need as a series of negatives: people feel depressed, feel disconnected, see 'nothing out there' and feel a library is 'not for me' and a course is unthinkable ('we'd walk right past'). Everyone who works in health and social care is aware that there is a crying need for work which will bring people together and offer opportunities for meaningful conversations and shared pleasure. I would like to see our project spread around the country in order to extend what books can offer still further.

At the time of writing Get Into Reading is working in partnership on Merseyside with two NHS trusts, and many social agencies, and we have over 350 weekly beneficiaries meeting to read together in small friendly groups. If we were to expand, could there be a new role for libraries as centres of social inclusion? Our experience on Merseyside seems to point to that possibility. It would be a wonderful thing to imagine each of Britain's 4515 public libraries hosting a GIR group once a week: what an enormous social resource that would be for people with mental or other health problems, for homeless people, for young mothers feeling isolated and adrift, for carers desperate for serious fun. I hope that library workers will take up the challenge offered above by Jill: 'Just get out there and try something.'

I also hope that librarians will learn, from some of the readers in this chapter, not to fear the great books which are our literary heritage but to begin to see them as 'foul-weather friends' – a resource to turn to in times of human difficulty. Of course our literary education does not help – sadly, nothing is more likely to make a book unreal than studying it for 'A' level or 'doing' it as an undergraduate on a theory-dominated university course. The courageous readers featured in this article all talk about the pleasure, satisfaction and sense of meaning they have gained by reading not just 'books' but also 'literature' – great writing, including the world's greatest-ever writers, Shakespeare and Tolstoy. Let's all get into reading, not for examination purposes but for personal pleasure and development. Let's use literature as writers intend – for ourselves.

Bibliography

Blake, William, 'The Tyger'. In *Songs of Innocence and Experience*
Brighouse, Harold, *Hobson's Choice*
Brontë, Charlotte, *Jane Eyre.*
Brontë, Emily, *Wuthering Heights*
Dahl, Roald, *Charlie and the Chocolate Factory*
Dickens, Charles, *The Adventures of Oliver Twist*
Durrell, Gerald, *My Family and Other Animals*
Eliot, George, *Adam Bede*
Grahame, Kenneth, *The Wind in The Willows*
Hines, Barry, *Kes: a play of the novel*
Hoban, Russell, 'Schwarz'. In *Encounter*
Lawrence, D. H., *Sons and Lovers*
Milton, John, *Paradise Lost*
Norton, Mary, *The Borrowers*
Piercy, Marge, *Woman on the Edge of Time*
Priestley, J. B., *An Inspector Calls: a play in three acts*
Richardson, Samuel, *Clarissa or the history of a young lady*
Russ, Joanna, *The Female Man*
Shakespeare, William, *Macbeth*
Shakespeare, William, *Measure for Measure*

Shakespeare, William, *Romeo and Juliet*

Shakespeare, William, *Sonnets*

Shakespeare, William, *The Winter's Tale*

Spyri, Johanna, *Heidi*

Steinbeck, John, *Of Mice and Men*

Tales from the Arabian Nights, selected from the book *A Thousand Nights and a Night,* translated and annotated by Sir Richard Burton

Tennyson, Alfred, 'Crossing the Bar'. In *Demeter and Other Poems*

Thomas, Dylan, *Under Milk Wood: a play for voices*

Tolkien, J. R. R., *The Hobbit*

Tolstoy, Leo, *The Death of Ivan Ilych and Other Stories*

Wain, John, *Strike the Father Dead*

Woolf, Virginia, *Orlando: a biography.*

Note

1   Alfred Lord Tennyson, *Demeter and Other Poems*, London, Macmillan, 1889.

Section 3
Works of imagination

Introduction: Section 3

This section examines works of imagination and their impact, and developing ways of accessing them.

The first chapter in this section investigates the concept of rewriting existing stories as hypertext works. This process, among other things, provides the reader with the possibility of selecting multiple endings to works of literature. It explains the technical and literary issues involved in this process and uses the author's hypertext rewriting of *Dr Jekyll and Mr Hyde* to illustrate the possibilities.

This is followed by a consideration of the ways in which a new genre of futuristic fiction for young readers, more specifically for teenagers, has emerged since the late 1960s. The authorial premise is that young people today want to know about the dire consequences of human behaviours, and that they wish to address their fears for the future through reading dystopian-type fiction. This chapter provides a fascinating insight into an increasingly popular fiction genre.

The final contribution is by an established working poet and performer. He earns his living writing, publishing and presenting his work anywhere and everywhere it is possible to do so. Life as a full-time writer and performer, although very challenging, can be very rewarding. In this uplifting chapter he takes us through a diarized period in his life and includes a number of his poems for good measure.

Chapter 6

Two worlds collide: hypertext and rewriting

CALUM KERR

Editors' preface

With the age of computers and the world wide web we have developed new ways of reading. Internet users have become used to reading short sections of text, linked by hypertext to other related sections of text, and being able to make decisions about what sections they read. This provides readers with choice and control over their own reading paths and directions.

A new form of literature has developed that takes advantage of the changes in how we navigate texts. These 'hypertexts' form the basis of one possible future for literature, combining the old techniques of narrative creation with new technological methods of dissemination. This chapter examines the phenomenon of hypertexts, how we interact with them and how they affect us as both readers and writers. It investigates the possibility of alternative routes through, and perspectives on, a story.

The hypertext referred to in this chapter, *The Multiple Perspectives of Jekyll and Hyde*, is available online at www.jekyllandhyde-multipleperspectives. co.uk.

Introduction

As a lifelong student of creative writing, choosing a topic for my PhD was naturally a difficult thing to do. With the whole range of the written word open to me, where could I start and how could I ensure I would choose something of a sufficiently academic level? After much thought and consultation with tutors, I decided to combine a number of my interests by rewriting a classic gothic story as a computer-driven web of texts known as a *hypertext*. In doing this I would be obliged to examine not just the process of writing, but also that of rewriting. I would need to combine this with a study of hypertext and the interaction with this new medium of both writer and reader. A lot of work had already been done on the theory and practice of hypertext, and more still on the processes of both writing and rewriting, but there had been little investigation of the crossover between these two fields.

The survival of any new medium – be it the replacement of LPs with CDs or VHS tapes with DVDs – lies partly in its ability to provide adaptations of previous works. This must hold true for the medium of the literary hypertext if it is to become more than just a curiosity. To investigate the possibilities for this, I chose to rework R. L. Stevenson's *The Strange Case of Dr Jekyll and Mr Hyde* as a narrative in hypertext form, with all the implications of this in terms of increased accessibility and navigability which 'new media' can bring.

This led to two areas of consideration: first, the concept of hypertext itself – what it is, how it works and how readers interact with it; second, the process of rewriting itself and how the use of the new medium affects this process. In this chapter I will look at the theories surrounding these areas and explore how they were applied in the actual writing of the hypertext, which became *The Multiple Perspectives of Jekyll and Hyde*.

What is hypertext?

The word 'hypertext' was originally coined by Ted Nelson in 1965, in his book *Literary Machines*. He defined the term as 'nonsequential writing—text that branches and allows choice to the reader, best read at an interactive screen. As popularly conceived, this is a series of text chunks connected by links which offer the reader different pathways'.

A more recent entry from *The Electronic Labyrinth* defines hypertext as 'the presentation of information as a linked network of nodes which readers are free to navigate in a non-linear fashion. It allows for multiple authors, a blurring of the author and reader functions, extended works with diffuse boundaries, and multiple reading paths' (Keep et al., n.d.). This second definition contains a number of key terms, which are worth listing as they will inform any discussion on hypertext and its importance. These are: linked network, nodes, non-linear, blurring of the author and reader functions, diffuse boundaries and multiple reading paths. These are useful concepts and help to define the crucial distinction between an electronic text and a hypertext.

An electronic text is the closest computerized relative of a paper-based text. One common form of this is the e-book, whereby a paper-based text can be read on screen. The reader can access the different sections via the contents page, and has the ability to turn from one page to another. However, the work is structurally no different from its paper-based counterpart and allows the reader no interactivity with the text beyond that which is already available from the physical object. In order to be a hypertext, a text must demonstrate the nodal and non-sequential features mentioned, the ability to link from each 'page' to a number of other 'pages', and for a number of other 'pages' (though not necessarily the same pages) to link back. Of course, this nodal structure is not solely the province of computerization (Aarseth, 1997, 14), but increasing usage of computers – and more particularly the internet – has associated it more with the computer than with any other form.

As George Landow points out in the introduction to his 1997 book *Hypertext 2.0*, most definitions of hypertext and its methods of creation and interpretation are reminiscent of Roland Barthes describing an 'ideal textuality' in *S/Z*:

> [T]he networks are many and interact, without any one of them being able to surpass the rest; this text is a galaxy of signifiers, not a structure of signifieds; it has no beginning, it is reversible; we gain access to it by several entrances, none of which can be authoritatively declared to be the main one . . ., the systems of meaning can take over this absolutely plural text, but their number is never closed, based as it is on the infinity of language.
>
> (Barthes, 2002, 5–6)

Barthes's suggestion is that it would be preferable to have a more amorphous approach to text and that written text should be able to engage in activities more traditionally associated with oral cultures: the chance to ramble, sidetrack and backtrack. However, Landow's use of this quote does not quite fit the case, as hypertext, while striving to be this ideal text, has not yet achieved this status. Barthes continues:

> [F]or the plural text, there cannot be a narrative structure, a grammar, or a logic; thus, if one or another of these are sometimes permitted to come forward, it is in proportion . . . as we are dealing with incompletely plural texts whose plural is more or less parsimonious.
>
> (Barthes, 2002, 6)

In other words, the 'ideal' text – the 'absolutely plural' text – can never be realized. All that we can hope to achieve is a partial reflection of such a text.

Hypertext realities

The above passages were written by Barthes as part of a quasi-Platonic attempt to understand how 'real' texts work by positing the characteristics of an 'ideal' text. This ideal text he termed a 'writerly' text – one in which the reader is 'no longer a consumer, but a producer of the text'. Against this, he discussed the 'readerly' text, which contains that which 'can be read, but not written' (Barthes, 2002, 4). This distinction between the two types of text is useful when referring to hypertext. If the writerly text is one in which the reader is changed from consumer to producer, then it is a text within which the reader engages in a collaborative effort with the absent writer – a perfect way of describing the way in which readers of a hypertext must construct their own pathway through the blocks of text – known as 'lexias'[1] – which make up the hypertext.

However, despite the multiplicity of links and nodes in a hypertext, there will always be a preformatted structure imposed by the writer. Readers are channelled and controlled by the structure imposed by the hypertext's creator, no matter how much control these readers may have over their interaction with the text.

In writing for print, the 'hardware' is the book and the 'software' is the reader's ability to read, and these are (within certain limits) constant. However, with hypertext the hardware and software can vary immensely, to the extent that no two writers or readers are likely to have access to exactly the same technical facilities. Care must be taken not to exclude readers from accessing the hypertext. The frustration felt by readers excluded by the need to use one of the many 'e-book' readers or proprietary hypertext engines is comparable to that felt by those trying unsuccessfully to access websites that require the user to have the latest version of a web browser or a special 'plug-in'.

Hypertexts, HTML and cybertexts

To this end, more and more hypertexts are being created in HTML, which is the standard language used across the world wide web, and design principles from the web design industry are being taken into account, in order to maximize the number of browsers and operating systems that can access each hypertext.

Certain of these design factors to have emerged from web design arise from the concept of what the reader of a hypertext is and is not willing to do. In my other life as a web designer, factors such as download time and the resistance of readers to scrolling through pages and pages of text have become predominant. This has led to the production of short pages (the 'lexias' mentioned earlier), which use a large number of links to other pages, making full use of the networking features of the medium. In this way, and many others, the nature of writing for hypertext has evolved its own set of standards and practices distinct from those required for print.

The size of the lexias, and the interwoven way in which they are arranged, form a grammar of their own. The ability to link different blocks of texts in unexpected or multiple ways gives the author a chance to suggest layers of meaning, not from the text itself but from the way the blocks within the text are combined. This differs from print text in that different connotations can be created from each new pathway. This is important in terms of narrative. With the concepts of beginnings, endings and plot in flux, the result is a text which can be seen as more of a gestalt than a linear narrative.

This is a theme echoed by Espen J. Aarseth in his 1997 book *Cybertext*, in which he discusses ideas about what makes a hypertext different from a traditional printed text. He suggests that there are problems with the two main ways of looking at hypertexts - either as straightforward extensions of written texts, using all the same literary and critical theories, or as a completely new form of literature for which new rules need to be created (Aarseth, 1997, 14). His contention is that the difference is one of function rather than substance, and that the theories of both literature and computers are applicable to hypertexts.

Aarseth uses the term 'cybertexts' to encompass both written hypertexts and more dynamic texts such as computer games. This conflation of forms in his account allows him to include written forms analogous to hypertexts (e.g. Vladimir Nabokov's *Pale Fire*, 2000; Italo Calvino's *If On a Winter's Night a Traveller*, 1998) and analyse them alongside computer-based hypertexts.

This allows for a crucial idea as regards the difference between hypertext and standard paper-based texts, and that is the 'journey' taken by the reader. To this end, Aarseth uses the model of the labyrinth.

Mazes and labyrinths

Early mazes or labyrinths were unicursal – that is, they had a single path. You entered at the entrance, walked leisurely round the inside of the maze, and found yourself at a bench or other feature at the centre. Then, after a short break, you walked back until you were out again. If nothing else it provided a long walk in a small area. This is directly comparable to what is normally understood as a text. You enter at the beginning with the first page, then you trace the only path available to you by turning each page as you reach its end, and starting on the next one. Finally, you reach the end and you shut the book.[2] This is a unicursal text.

A multicursal labyrinth is of the type more familiar in modern times – the labyrinth of Theseus and the Minotaur.[3] Here there may be a number of entrances, and there is no single path through the maze. There may be many different paths, all leading to different exits, and there will also be many optional paths and dead-ends. This is a useful model for a literary hypertext. There are many points at which the reader can enter, and many points at which they can choose which part of the narrative to pursue. This level of choice, unlike in the standard novel, does not even need to take place on a page-by-page basis, but can be as granular as word by word. Finally, there are links which take the reader to sidebars to the text but no further, and cause them to retrace their steps and find another path through the maze. This is a multicursal text, a hypertext (Aarseth, 1997, 5-7).

This is a useful distinction and brings us back again to Barthes's idea of the reader's interaction being necessary in the creation of writerly texts. The presence of dead-ends and multiple entrances and exits to a text call attention to the text itself and involve the reader. This interactivity, as Marie-Laure Ryan discusses in her article on the subject (Ryan, 2001), works against the process of immersion. In contrast, the fact that different facets of the narrative can be explored in great detail allows for an increased level of immersion and renders the text more readerly. Therefore, the degree to which a text can be seen as readerly or writerly, within our new, limited definitions of the terms, will depend on the ease of use of the interface and how much it is foregrounded in the production of the hypertext.

When I set out to write *The Multiple Perspectives* I had to take this into account both in its interface – the screen presented to the reader – and in its structure. It is a nodal work that allows readers to browse, in a non-linear fashion, the four narratives of the main characters. The nodes form at points of confluence between the narratives, allowing the reader to trace a single narrative path through the text from a beginning to an ending. The path taken is dependent on the decisions of the reader, and allows them to take side-trips into the narratives of minor characters before returning to the main thread. It fulfils the classic definitions of a hypertext while also using the ideas and innovations developed for the internet and for computer games to create a text which can be both writerly and immersive.

How do we read and write a hypertext?

The main problem in examining how to read or write a hypertext, as Landow comments in *Hypertext 2.0*, is that our principles of reading and understanding any kind of text are based on print technology (Landow, 1997, 57). To this end it is important to understand how a literary text is approached, in any form, before moving on to literary hypertext as the specific case.

In his 1980 collection *Is There a Text in this Class?* Stanley Fish brings together a number of his essays on the nature of a text and its interpretation. Across the essays, written over a number of years, he looks at aspects of how meaning within texts is constructed in a tension formed between the author's intentions and the reader's interpretation. While his writings were aimed at understanding texts created for print, many of his points are applicable to hypertext.

His focus is on the reader inasmuch as, to the reader, the author's intentions are unknown, and the only source for interpretation of the text is the reader's knowledge and experience. Meaning must therefore be produced by the interpretation of the reader alone. However, he also counters that the reader's possible interpretations are constrained by the text and by the way the author has created structures within it.

In 'Interpreting the Variorum', Fish (1980, 147-73) brings these two arguments together. He does this by reconciling his previous formalist approach, where meaning was seen to exist in the nature of the work itself, with his ideas of reader-response analysis. He then applies a formalist approach to two short passages from Milton's poem *Lycidas*, where meaning and its production are seen as emerging from the structure of the poem and the ordering of words, lines and thoughts within it. Thus, he shows that interpretation of the text is independent of the reader's experience of it. The meaning in this case is seen as having been created prior to the reader's interaction with the text, and is a result of the formal structures within it. However, he develops the argument further to show that these formal units are only present within the text because the construction of a formalist model is based upon certain assumptions of what a unit comprises and so are 'a function of the interpretative model one brings to bear' (Fish, 1980, 164). He then extends this theory to cover intentions as well, stating that they do not proceed from the author, who realizes them in the formal structure of the text, but are a product of the reader's interpretation. Only in the process of perception or interpretation, says Fish, can formal units and intention be identified. This allows for an understanding of the reading of a text that includes the physical process itself. Meaning within a text is, in this case, as much a product of the reader's movement through the text – both in time and in space – as it is a product of the text itself as a static object (Fish, 1980, 165).

Hypertext relationships

This leads us back to our examination of hypertext. The relation of lexias to each other, both spatially (i.e. the links from one lexia to a series of others) and chronologically (i.e. the time it takes a reader to move from any one lexia to any other, whether due to the structure of the hypertext or as a result of linking choices by the reader), is crucial in the way hypertext works. The very purpose of many hypertexts is to create interpretative frameworks which exist outside of the text, encouraging the reader to create meaning from interrelation that cannot exist without the intervention of the reader. However, these relations are still a product of the writer's intentions and so the problem of determining whether meaning is constructed by the author or by the reader remains.

Interpretive communities

Fish explains that just as the formal structures which can be identified in a text are ultimately a product of a process of interpretation, so are the strategies that a reader uses to interpret meaning within a text. These strategies pre-exist the reader, creating the shape of what is read. Thus, Fish invokes the idea of 'interpretive communities': notional groups of individuals who share the same interpretative strategies and therefore interpret similar texts in the same way, with meaning still being generated from the act of reading rather than from the text. As texts will also be produced within such a community, the role of the author is one of interpretation, and creation occurs using the community's interpretative strategies (Fish, 1980, 167-73). This forms a cycle, with readers' interpretations feeding into writers' interpretations and back to readers again. This notion of interpretive communities is particularly useful in thinking about hypertext, where the level of reader feedback is much higher than in print media due to the accessibility of the writer and the propensity of readers to become writers themselves, working within their own communities.

This idea also illuminates a problem that emerges in the examination of the writing of hypertext – that different interpretive strategies are brought to bear by different interpretive communities. In the case of hypertext, there are two distinct groups with an interest, and, although there are many areas of overlap, those using hypertext for literary purposes and those exploring the nature of nodal documents within a computer-science framework have very different agendas. These two communities would read the same hypertext in different ways, and would create different meanings within them. As a result, a writer of hypertext must either be aware of which interpretive community they are a member and write for that community, or try to apply the interpretive strategies of both in the creation of text, thus stretching the limitations of Fish's theory to allow for the writer to be a member of more than one community at the same time. To use Fish's phrase, the writer of hypertext must apply an 'interpretation that is . . . aware of itself' (Fish, 1980, 167), and therefore aware of the communities to which it belongs. When writing a text, the author, acting within the same interpretive community(/ies) as the reader, is accessing the same set of interpretive strategies that the reader will employ to create their own meaning within the text.

The existence of these communities was demonstrated to me during testing for *The Multiple Perspectives*. I used two different groups for testing to reflect the two communities that hypertext spans. I asked two groups of students, one from a creative writing course and one from a web design course, to read through the hypertext and give me feedback on their experience. In a reflection of Fish's theories, the issues thrown up by the two groups were quite different. The web design students commented on layout, appearance, ease of navigation and perceived coding issues. They mentioned nothing about the story itself. Conversely, the creative writers pointed out my errors in spelling, grammar and narrative progression and took all the 'computery' things for granted. Between them they gave me a set of results that no one group could have produced. These were used to finalize the hypertext, helping it to be relevant to the two communities.

Why do we rewrite?

The revisiting of texts in other forms is not a new phenomenon. As Paul Cobley discusses in his book *Narrative* (Cobley, 2001, 29-55), the early forms of oral storytelling involved the retelling of the same stories over and over again. This 'bardic function', as he terms it (229), allowed a community's central narratives to be told back to it again and again in order to reinforce its mores and values. The same story might have been told over and over again with only minor changes, even something as simple as a change of inflection. However, this retelling process might also have involved the same motifs appearing in different situations and featuring different characters.

Beyond this idea of core stories which are retold within a community, there is the retelling of specific written texts - rewriting as it is understood today. However, again this is not new. Many of Shakespeare's plays are rewritings of earlier works, or the dramatizing of previously written histories, and Marlowe's *Doctor Faustus* was adapted from an English translation of a German chapbook.

However, the rewriting of *The Strange Case of Dr Jekyll and Mr Hyde* for the creation of *The Multiple Perspectives* was an explicit reworking of an earlier story, using the original text in varying degrees to create a new perspective. The reasons for this kind of 'borrowing' of the themes and features of an original text is often to examine opinions and attitudes not present in the original, or to use the tension created in the differences between the original and the rewritten as a critique of them both. In this way, the process of rewriting can be seen as a process of critical rereading.

Perhaps the most famous retelling of an earlier story is James Joyce's *Ulysses*, in which the long tale of Homer's *The Odyssey*[4] is compressed into a single day and reinterpreted within events in the lives of three Dubliners. *Ulysses* performs Cobley's 'bardic function' in that it reuses an earlier form to reinterpret a community's values. However, this retelling goes far beyond simple reaffirmation. The use of the original source within the title, and the compression of the timeline to a single day, show awareness within the text of its rewritten nature – an extra level of reference which is typical of the modernist mode within which Joyce was working.

While this kind of self-conscious rewriting can certainly be seen as a product of modernism, it is even more closely associated with those ideas which are usually termed 'postmodernism' (Cobley, 2001, 171–200). By re-using an original text openly, and declaring the fact of rewriting, the author performs 'rupturing', wishing the reader to accept both the tale and the fact that it is being told. This kind of rewritten work explicitly foregrounds the fact of its rewriting and must be examined in these terms. In addition, while hypertext fits to some extent with Barthes's idea of the ideal text (Barthes, 2002, 5–6), so any kind of rewriting can also be seen as an example of this idea. The process of rewriting embodies active interaction between the rewriter as reader and the original text: working with the signifiers of the original to connect them to new signifieds, and allowing the rewriter to write what the original author was unable to. In turn, by presenting a rewritten text and foregrounding its rewritten nature, the author forces readers into a dialogue between the two texts, asking them to form their own judgements and reach their own conclusions.

How do we rewrite?

First and foremost, the process of rewriting a text must be based on an understanding of the workings of the original. The story must first be disassembled into its component parts to see how it achieves its effects, before a reconstruction can take place.

In order to perform this disassembly, it is necessary to understand the parts that make up a narrative. There have been many attempts to classify the parts that make up a narrative. All make a distinction between the events from which the narrative is constructed, and the way in which these are related to the audience.

However, in rewriting it is necessary to go one step beyond this dual formulation, and use Paul Cobley's three-part concept of story–plot–narrative (Cobley, 2001, 4–7). In this system, the term 'story' refers to the linear series of events which occur. These are selected and rearranged, then related in the form of the narrative. The plot is the chain of causes and effects which link the various elements of the story together, and can expand to include anything the author desires – therefore allowing for retelling, rewritings and new narratives. Paul Cobley uses the example of *Oliver Twist*. In the original novel by Charles Dickens, the facts of Oliver's parenthood, and their bearing on all other events, are not revealed until very nearly the end of the book. In contrast, Cobley informs us:

> The 1999 television version . . . has a different narrative. The first episode of the four-part series consists of a detailed narration of the love affair between Oliver's parents. . . . This narrative not only moves the facts of their story to the beginning . . . but it also depicts the affair 'first-hand', with the characters speaking their own dialogue and acting out the events, rather than having them retold by 'Monks' and Leeford's friend, Brownlow.   (Cobley, 2001, 5)

Thus the narrative – the particular example of the telling of the story – can individuate the events of the story. Different narratives can 'show' events which were previously 'told' and vice versa.

Cobley then continues to outline another difference: 'The narrative of the TV version also has additions: the murder of Leeford and the continued existence through subsequent episodes of Leeford's wife' (Cobley, 2001, 5).

And so, in different examples of narrative, different moments from the larger series of events that make up the plot may be chosen to be incorporated into any single telling of the story, even such moments as were not encapsulated in the original version.

With Cobley's three-part scheme, the nature of rewritings – the different ways they handle the events of the story, and their method of retelling – can be understood. The rewriter can reconstruct the plot to form a new story, and then determine how the story will be communicated to the audience by the new narrative.

The rewriting of Stevenson's *Jekyll and Hyde*

There have been many versions of the story of Jekyll and Hyde – films, plays and graphic novels – and many allusions to the story within other works. However, most re-interpretations have introduced new elements into the plot, which either contradict the events of the original text or remove parts of the original plot which erase key points of the original. In doing this, the rewritten texts fail to attract the authority sought from using the original. New readers are not generally directed to the original text by such rewritings, and so there is none of the 'authority by association' that occurs in more considerate rewritings.

The Strange Case has been the subject of many diverse rewritings. As well as Valerie Martin's (2001) well-respected *Mary Reilly* – which works within the original plot – there have been films, plays, graphic novels, comedy sketches and so on which take the core themes from the plot – the ability to change one's physical form using a potion, and the notion of 'doubleness' (Motion, n.d.) – and jettison much of the rest. However, the extent to which a canonical text such as *The Strange Case* has entered popular culture means that it is perfect for a more straightforward and measured rewriting. Thanks to the distance that has been created between popular conceptions of the plot and the details of the original narrative, this original now has the power to surprise once more. This is what Martin relied upon in *Mary Reilly*, and what I relied upon in the writing of *The Multiple Perspectives*.

There is one more issue relating to rewriting *The Strange Case* which must be mentioned here: the relation between content and form in the rewriting. One of the main factors behind the decision to rewrite *The Strange Case* for this project was the nature of the story. It is the nature of a rewritten text to add to, and to some extent replace, the original. In many ways, this would serve as an apt description of Hyde's actions within the text – supplementing Jekyll's existence, and then ultimately replacing him. And so I decided to include Hyde's point of view in the retelling – something which never occurs in the original text. Thus, the rewritten text allows his voice to be heard. It is this addition of the voice of what is often termed 'the other' that makes the rewritten text substantially different from Robert Louis Stevenson's original.

In allowing 'the other' a voice, and by choosing to write his narrative both in the first person and in the present tense, the balance is shifted towards acceptance of 'the other' as real, human and of consequence. It forces the reader to deal with the problems which caused 'the other' to be excluded in the first place. This movement towards reader involvement in the story is, of course, not only central to the foregrounding of 'the other', but also part of the process of conversion to hypertext.

The effects of rewriting for hypertext

One of the liberating features of producing hypertext is that there is no need to use a standard linear narrative. However, the process of rewriting a text with a strong linear narrative re-imposes this constraint, so the process of developing the rewritten text for hypertext is one of seeing how far this constraint can be pushed: if the rewriter tries to take the alterations to the text too far they will lose their connection to the original text, and thus the associative process of rewriting becomes lost.

The definition of hypertext refers to it as nodal. Each lexia within the hypertext should link out to other lexias in a web-like, rather than linear, fashion. There are two ways to achieve this. One is to split the original text into lexias, and then link them in ways that achieve new progressions of the narrative, and therefore a different perspective on the text. However, this is not a rewriting but a re-configuring. The second way is to rewrite the text, creating new pathways, and linking between them.

Here, again, Aarseth's (1997) labyrinth metaphor is useful: there will be more than one straight path through the text, with side branches, some of which lead to other paths and some of which lead to dead-ends – a web with more than one beginning and more than one ending. As in this case the process is of rewriting a linear text, these paths are likely to follow a similar line to the original, but the ability to link between them, and to side narratives that do not follow the main line, makes it a true hypertext.

Having chosen to use hypertext for a rewriting, the author is obliged to produce many strands of narrative from the original. How this is done will, of course, depend on the writer and on the text chosen for rewriting. The creation of the new narrative involves creating several narratives which interweave and interrelate.

The rewriting process here involves the deconstruction and reconstruction process outlined earlier, focusing on the points of interaction, as these are the nodes which will form the structure of the hypertext. In this way, the process of reconstruction becomes twofold. First, new sections of plot must be constructed to outline what occurs to each of the characters during those times, as described in the original text, when they are apart. Second, the points of convergence must be reconstructed to represent differing interpretations of events by the different characters. The points of contact provide interest by revealing the differing thoughts of the protagonists involved, and still further interest is found in moving away along the narrative strand of one character or another to see what occurs.

An examination of the specific rewriting involved in this project shows that the fact of it being created for hypertext affects all stages of production, and, while limiting the form of the rewriting in some ways, provides avenues for experimentation that would not be possible in a paper-based text.

The Multiple Perspectives of Jekyll and Hyde

When constructing a narrative for hypertext, regardless of whether it is an original work or a rewriting, there is a constant need to be conscious that it is being created to be a hypertext. As a result it seemed natural to choose a story in which the main theme was one of duality – fitting the content to the form. There is a natural break in the text at the points at which Jekyll turns into Hyde. The formatting of the hypertext on the screen only adds to this, signalling the change to the reader. In gothic literature 'the other' is a constant presence, but the voice of 'the other' is rarely heard. The process of rewriting for hypertext not only allows 'the other' to be heard; the reader's expectations of the abilities of hypertext to provide information practically enforces it. The world of computers and the internet has created readers who expect information to be available and immediate. The form of hypertext accepts this and provides what is expected. The reader of such a text therefore expects to be able to access previously unavailable voices simply and easily.

My first task in the rewriting was to break the original narrative down into its individual components. This involved a close reading of the text to identify all of the different characters, the various scenes that they are each involved in and a timeline of events for each character – all written out on a very large piece of paper. Having discovered that there were actually 17 distinct characters in the original novella, and with a desire to finish writing the hypertext one day, I decided to concentrate on just four main characters.

However, during the processes of research and writing, I made the decision to engage with Aarseth's notion of a hypertext as a multicursal narrative, and the events surrounding some of the minor characters were reintroduced. Each minor character was incorporated as a small group of lexias, each with a particular connection back to the main story. Each lexia contains no links other than back to the main narrative, providing the dead-ends that occur in multicursal labyrinths, requiring the reader to double-back to the main path to continue the journey.

To accentuate the differences between the characters, and to reduce confusion in the reader when moving from one narrative to another, it was necessary to find individual 'voices' for the characters. I had already decided to write Hyde in the present tense with all other characters in the past tense, which immediately gave his voice a different tone. The other voices were all written in pseudo-Victorian language, utilizing the long sentences popular at the time of writing of *The Strange Case*, as well as some of the vocabulary.

The process of creating the plots involved deciding numerous timelines and which events needed to be dramatized and which merely mentioned. I decided to use concrete dates for the events of the narratives, in order to make navigation easier. This required a very close reading of the text to determine the dates of events as outlined by Stevenson. Finally, with the details of the plots for these characters in place, the process of writing and structuring could begin.

Two things were held in the forefront of my mind at all times. First, the story would have to be split into lexias small enough to fit onto a computer screen with the minimum of scrolling, so events should be related in a way which would achieve this. Second, links would be created at the point of character interactions, so these should be constructed to allow for seamless movement between narratives, and to create interest because of the differences between them. Within such a structure, there are two main types of event: events that occur in only one narrative strand, and events that occur in more than one narrative strand but are perceived differently by the various protagonists.

Finally, three minor characters were chosen to act as dead-ends. These were the characters that I felt had the most new information to provide: the girl who is trampled by Hyde and whose tale opens the original novella, the maid who witnesses the murder of Sir Danvers Carew and the hotel attendant who provides for Hyde on the day Jekyll changes unbidden into him.

Thus, it was possible for me to create four narratives which interweave. The reader can choose which one to follow, and then change between them using a structure of interaction based on a physical, three-dimensional model of the world as a story. In the same way that a film director chooses which character to follow, the reader of the hypertext can choose who to follow after any of the nodes. It allows the reader to continue with the main narrative or to move behind the scenes to view the events unfolding for the other characters, in a similar fashion to that used by Tom Stoppard in

Rosencrantz and Guildenstern are Dead. The main difference here is that both options are open to the reader, and one does not exclude the other. In this way, the hypertext is similar to the first-person computer games where different routes may be taken and different information obtained, but narrative continues to flow in a coherent fashion.

Conclusion

The Multiple Perspectives, as stated earlier, is a product of constraints on both the hypertext and the rewriting, each caused by the other. However, the result is a true hypertext – one in which the structure is nodal and it is the interaction between the lexias, and the reader's individual navigation of them, which creates the story – which still manages to ape the structure of traditional, linear, paper-based fiction. As a result, it could be said that *The Multiple Perspectives* does not represent the future of the hypertext. This is more likely to result from work within the computer games industry. However, it does provide a way in for the 'ordinary' reader who would normally be wary of the possible confusion and navigation problems often encountered with the more experimental hypertexts. The result is readable and easily navigable, and yet still uses the innovative processes that make hypertext such an interesting and exciting medium.

As a project, *The Multiple Perspectives* was intended to appeal to both the literary and computer-science communities. To some extent it has both succeeded and failed, but it is surely representative of the desire present in both these communities to find a way to work together. It is perhaps a precursor of projects involving writers and programmers to produce virtual environments that the reader can explore, without constantly being judged as winning or losing, as experienced in most computer games. It is a way forward into a world where immediacy and interaction are increasingly desired, and demonstrates a way for readers and writers to work together.

However, as well as answering most of the questions initially posed in the proposal for this project, the process has also illuminated areas for future research. Until now, computers have largely been used to imitate other processes. At first, computers were used to replace the abacus and the calculator as mathematical machines. Then, they were used to replace the typewriter, the filing cabinet and, with the advent of e-mail, the memo and the letter. Finally, with the arrival of the internet, they are starting to replace the television and the radio. What this shows is that the computer is good at modelling other processes. However, one thing it does not model well is the book. The problems of portability and poor screen resolution are well known, and due to the widespread use of the internet, a simple paper-to-computer conversion is seen as needless and unsophisticated.

Future research needs to address the ways in which the computer can be moved on from simply modelling existing artefacts to bringing together its various abilities to create a new form of narrative experience. Whether this lies in the realm of the literary or of the computer game remains to be seen but, with a generation growing up who turn more naturally to a computer for both information and entertainment than to a book, it is certainly an area that needs to be explored, with greater co-operation between the communities involved.

Bibliography

Aarseth, E. J. (1997) *Cybertext*, Johns Hopkins University Press.

Barthes, R. (2002) *S/Z*, Blackwell Publishing.

Calvino, I. (1998) *If On a Winter's Night a Traveller*, Vintage.

Cobley, P. (2001) *Narrative*, The New Critical Idiom Series, Routledge.

Fish, S. (1980) *Is There a Text in this Class?*, Harvard University Press.

Joyce, J. (1997) *Ulysses*, Everyman's Library.

Keep, C., McLaughlin, T. and Parmar, R. (n.d.) *The Electronic Labyrinth*,
     www.iath.virginia.edu/elab/hfl0037.html [accessed 11 February 2004].

Landow, G. P.(1997) *Hypertext 2.0*, Johns Hopkins University Press.

Martin, V. (2001) *Mary Reilly*, Vintage Contemporaries.

Motion, A. (n.d.) *Andrew Motion discusses Robert Louis Stevenson's* The Strange
     Case of Dr Jekyll and Mr Hyde,
     www.penguin.co.uk/shared/webdisplay/1,,213620_1_10,00.html?cs=10
     [accessed 9 September 2004].

Nabakov, V. (2000) *Pale Fire*, Penguin.

Nelson, T. (1982) *Literary Machines*, Mindful Press, quote taken from
     http://virtual.park.uga.edu/%7ehypertxt/ht2.html [accessed 11 February
     2004].

Ryan, M.-L. (2001) *Narrative as Virtual Reality: immersion and interactivity in
     literature and electronic media*, Johns Hopkins University Press.

Stevenson, R. L. (1998) *The Strange Case of Dr Jekyll and Mr Hyde*, Oxford
     University Press.

Stoppard, T. (1976) *Rosencrantz and Guildenstern Are Dead: a play*, Samuel French.

Notes

1   The blocks of text making up a hypertext - words, lines, paragraphs, pages, or chapters - are generally termed 'lexias' in accordance with Barthes's idea of 'units of reading': 'The lexia will include sometimes a few words, sometimes several sentences; it will be a matter of convenience: it will suffice that the lexia be the best possible space in which we can observe meanings' (Barthes, 2002, 5-6). While the word 'lexia' is itself plural, it is most commonly used in the singular with the word 'lexias' serving as the plural. This convention will be followed in the rest of this work.

2   This is a very specific and simplified model of reading.

3   Although there is some argument about whether Theseus's labyrinth was unicursal or multicursal (Aarseth, 1997, 6), this is not relevant here.

4   This was itself originally a product of an oral culture. Homer himself is even believed by many to be the invention of a culture requiring a single author for what is in effect a collaboration of many poets over many years.

Chapter 7

Dire consequences?: the development of futuristic fiction as a genre for young readers

KAY SAMBELL

Editors' preface

Tacit theories about childhood and youth are a crucial but challenging area with which professionals working with and for young people routinely engage. This chapter will enable professionals to consider their own values, attitudes and assumptions about the varying views of childhood, youth and literacy that underpin the emergence of a bleak, dystopian literature for young readers. The genre and its critical reception foregrounds and frequently calls into question some stock assumptions adults often hold about the nature of childhood and about young readers as a group. In this way it acts as a useful springboard for thinking about approaches to professional practice.

Introduction

When I first studied authors' use of future fictional time in the mid-1990s, I discovered, rather to my surprise, that it was much easier to find evidence of fears for the future of our young within children's literature and its criticism, than it was to find examples of the various anodyne futures that were envisaged by the social theorists of the time (Frankel, 1987). Writers of, and commentators on, books for the young tended to believe that technological 'progress' was more likely to result in harm, and to undermine traditionally cherished human values, than to become a benign force. As a rule distress about the future appeared to make the idea of a literary utopia seem like a naïve dream, and a dark dystopian literature for teenagers emerged. Since then, the immense popularity of this genre shows little sign of abating, and the list of titles produced steadily lengthens each year, although, as I will suggest by the end of the chapter, it has recently begun to develop in new ways, becoming increasingly adventurous, richly textured and experimental.

It is particularly noteworthy that futuristic fiction for young readers has emerged in the context of deep public anxiety about growing up. Quite simply, this genre articulates deep-seated fears about the world – what it has become and what that might imply for the future of childhood and adolescence. It reveals considerable evidence of a growing sense of an imagined historical crisis of unprecedented proportions. Moreover, the fact that so many writers not only feel fearful about the future but also seek to engage young readers with their daunting, often horrifying speculations itself offers insight into dominant discourses about childhood and youth. Books produced with a young readership in mind do not just comment on social and political issues directly, but also powerfully embody adults' prevailing values, attitudes and assumptions towards young people as a group.

In what follows I will explore some of the dilemmas with which authors grapple when working with such dark material, drawing attention to the ways in which writers' constructions of the implied young reader's needs, tastes, levels of literary competence and so on appear to impact on the ways in which the stories are told. This genre is particularly important because it acutely highlights a host of fascinating tensions, questions, issues, dilemmas and challenges which, in general terms, surround the production, consumption, promotion and critical reception of all literature for young readers.

My argument is that, in very broad terms and with notable exceptions, books produced between the 1960s and the mid-1990s typically relied heavily on Orwell's *1984* (1949) and Huxley's *Brave New World* (1932) as the dominant genre models. Authors tended to adapt and compromise these classic adult dystopias in order to address a young readership. Without wishing to undermine its importance, in my view a fairly didactic, problematic literature emerged. In the earliest sections of this chapter I will demonstrate how authors struggled with the dystopian form, tending to over-control and spoil their stories.

The past decade, though, has started to see the emergence of a radical new set of futuristic texts. Authors are beginning to experiment with fresh themes, imagining, for example, astounding future blends of human and machine which radically reconfigure the status and nature of their young protagonists. They are also experimenting with adventurous narrative blends, mixing the classic dystopian vision with tropes from science fiction and horror in order to unlock innovative literary forms that appear equal to the new demands of our rapidly changing age.

The emergence of an imagined sense of historical crisis

It is not hard to see why authors began to depart radically from the optimistic confidence and outlook of the juvenile futuristic works of the 1950s and early 1960s. Broadly speaking, world events appeared to threaten the institution of childhood itself (Alberghene, 1985; Plotz, 1988). The atom bomb, for example, had swiftly ended the ravages of a world war, raising hopes that peace and liberty were attainable and that children could now inherit their benefits and refuse to make the same mistakes again. However, it also began to raise daunting and paralysing fears about human nature and its ability to control such lethal technology in the future, precipitating grave concerns about the world that children would inherit. By the 1970s it was becoming clear to the public imagination that the human race could now conceivably damage the environment on a scale that had previously seemed unimaginable. If the future looked bleak in the 1970s, in the past decade media coverage of the 9/11 attacks, computer viruses, terrorism, environmental disaster, debates about 'designer babies' and moral panics about the detrimental influences of media on young lives has escalated, rather than assuaged, the sense of pessimism and anxiety about impending 'technology-wrought misery' (Crew, 2004, 203).

In recent decades seemingly unprecedented advances in science and technology have impinged on all aspects of life. Many writers use future fictional time to raise questions about the ways in which science will be utilized in a future political or social context. They apparently respond to widespread fears that social values and common goals are currently disintegrating, as we face life in a changed world (Engdahl, 1980, 427). Many describe the 'void' or 'vacuum' which young people now face (Westall, 1979, 35). The fear that the good old days have gone and we must find a new course is commonly expressed (Egoff, 1969, 433; see also Alberghene, 1985, 188-93; Eakin, 1973, 320).

The view prevails (among children's writers and critics alike) that young people's needs will not be well-served by sheltering them too much from the occasionally painful truth (Steele, 1973, 288–97). The dystopia simply seems more realistic, given the current outlook and sensibility. Many also feel that because adults no longer feel confident that they know how to advise children to ensure their future happiness, juvenile books can no longer offer a nostalgic and comforting picture.

A literature of warning

As a result, bleak and shocking future worlds started to emerge for young readers from the late 1960s. I do not wish to suggest that there is anything purposefully gratuitous about the levels of horror and violence that pervade this grim literature of the future. Writers are primarily disposed to use the dystopian element of their fictions to challenge young readers, encouraging them to question and reject morally undesirable human actions. In this genre authors generally 'extrapolate from contemporary western reality to envisage a future world whose dystopic features are terrible exaggerations of the social, political, ecological, technological and biological present' in order to warn (Scutter, 1996, 4).

The genre is, then, fundamentally underpinned by the authorial premise that young people today need to know about the dire consequences of human behaviours, rather than be sheltered in a protective enclave of ignorance and innocent idealism. As Johnny Online in Thorpe's *Hybrids* puts it:

> Don't you realise what you're up against? You seem to think this is like some comic book adventure and you're superheroes. Instead, it's just a bunch of sad, scared and dangerous people running around and smashing into each other, causing damage cos they didn't think through the consequences of what they were doing.   (Thorpe, 2007, 245)

Admonitory literature is typically regarded as having a dual purpose. I write with the firm conviction that futuristic pessimism is not designed to depress or dispirit its young readers. Like all warning literature, I believe it is underpinned by the clear impulse to make people good by choice. Futuristic books are, as Harrison (1987, 86) says of Huxley and Orwell's dystopian fiction, 'calls of the imagination to the ethical'. They use their pessimistic frame of reference to assert that, for the reader, it is not too late.

Even though some writers may, at heart, seriously doubt humanity's ability to change, they frequently hope to suggest the possibility of something better in moral terms for their young readers.

Some common dystopian themes and preoccupations

Like in the classic adult dystopias, the centrepieces of many of the children's futuristic novels that began to emerge in the 1970s were political or technological. Frequently the main narrative interest was fuelled by the contrast between a small group of non-conformist children who were set against a repressive, intolerant and hyper-conformist body politic. Books that stressed the dramatic escalation of technology began to be produced in vast numbers. They depicted urban hells that made conditioned life intolerable, whether by overt fear and force like Orwell imagined, or by making citizens depressingly happy as in Huxley's world.

John Christopher became an early pioneer of the genre. In *The Guardians* (1970) he envisages a future in which people are dominated by a secret human elite of Guardians. His approach – the use of intentionally convincing, extrapolatory warning, which is so realistic it could be taken as a prediction – is typical of the approach taken by most children's writers subsequently to convey the awful implications of a stable future society. The didactic message was near the surface, with a sense of tight authorial control throughout, clearly guiding the reader's thoughts and presenting rather wooden characters who act as mouthpieces for the main ideas. According to John Rowe Townsend (1971), although it won the *Guardian* Award the socio-political framework of Christopher's novel is so obtrusive and simplistically conceived that it results in a spoilt story.

From the 1970s onwards, however, this formula attracted a vast number of children's writers. Many futuristic stories foreground a patently unjust and divisive future social system, arguably to the point of cliché. Strict class divisions are enforced in, for example, *Red Zone* (Browne, 1980), *Futuretrack 5* (Westall, 1983), *The Vandal* (Schlee, 1979), *Daz 4 Zoe* (Swindells, 1990), *King Creature Come* (Townsend, 1980), *The Tomorrow City* (Hughes, 1978), *Natfact 7* (Tully, 1984), *The Others* (Prince, 1986), *The Game* (Richemont, 1990), *Devil on My Back* (Hughes, 1984) and *This Time of Darkness* (Hoover, 1980). All of these books depict some version 'of a high-tech metropolis or bunker devoid of any positive life qualities' (Stephens, 1992, 128).

Sometimes the state fuels people's aggression by deliberately engineering extreme social divisions which make the privileged few jealously and selfishly guard their possessions. In some novels appalling institutionalized social deprivation is used, as in *1984*, to control the masses. People betray each other or clash in violent confrontation, or their anger erupts into vandalism and displays of destructive aggression.

Other texts choose to emphasize the fact that although superficially people are not openly hostile, and accept the enforced social inequality, they nevertheless feel no affection for each other. They are, like the inhabitants of Huxley's future world, merely cogs in a social machine. Often the computer is used to represent mindless conformity or silent violence that the people are powerless to resist. 'Infopaks' are inserted on the necks of the children in *Devil on My Back* (Hughes, 1984), so that their minds are docile and dominated by technology. In many books a secret human elite exploits science to control others' existence and people are only seen as numbers. Brainwashing is common, and drugs are often administered to pacify the population.

The concrete bunkers of the numerous dome cities or artificially lit underground bunkers clearly signal that this is not living, but merely existing. Frequently the inflexibility of the system is underlined by pitting the unyielding artificial concrete of the city against the fragile beauty of nature. In these worlds children have 'lost' their childhoods. The concept of childhood here is underpinned by a traditional Romantic discourse which sets it in cultural opposition to adulthood: a time of innocence, play and close affinity with nature. In short, the depiction of dystopian worlds is often crude and characterized by heavy-handed and over-worn devices to depict this 'loss'. The schematic and clichéd landscapes I am sketching here illustrate the prominence of the 'gadgetry' to which many writers resort, presumably to ensure that any reader can see the undesirability of the futures depicted.

The problems of adapting the dystopia for young readers

Many children's writers seem to be compelled to adapt the classic dystopia fundamentally when writing for children. Most display a tone of confidence and reassurance in the *denouement*, which does not exist in the classic adult versions. This is largely carried by the suggestion of an ultimate return to the normality from which the dystopian scenario has departed.

Thus, despite the seriousness of the issues being raised, the conclusions of many stories could be seen as facile and bogus, contradicting the admonitory impetus of the preceding text. For example, Mick and Lucy overthrow the state and the masses are finally free to find their families at the end of *The Game* (Richemont, 1990), and John departs to join an idyllic community at the end of *The Awakening Water* (Kesteven, 1997), being advised benignly: 'You've seen it can work. Now make sure that it does.'

A key feature of the dystopian novel for children, then, became the damaging implausibility of the protagonist's evasion of the dire consequences of the dystopia in which s/he is cast. The lucky escape that Kesteven imagines for John was repeated time and again. For example, Swindells' (1990) hero, Daz, has an unbelievably lucky escape when he is suddenly rescued by the police when about to be tortured and executed by a murderous gang of vandals. Rabbit and Tia in Hoover's (1973) *Children of Morrow* are fortunately rescued from maltreatment at the hands of the primitive Base society into which they were born. In Tom Browne's *Red Zone* (1980) Slagerman, the hero's brutal assailant, is run over by a truck just as he is about to slaughter Clem. In Hughes' (1978) *The Tomorrow City*, the omnipotent computer C3, which has 'rationalized' the city until hospitals close and euthanasia is commonly practised, happily destroys itself when it accidentally shoots Caro (whom it was programmed to protect), blinding but luckily not killing her.

I am not trying to suggest that these texts are anything but deeply committed to raising serious questions about human organizations, but simply highlighting the ludicrous implausibility of the dystopian protagonist, as Romantic hero, being saved or reformed. I believe that the frequency with which some very accomplished children's writers resort to this strategy is actually designed to provide a balanced view or solution within the narrative itself, rather than trusting the young reader to supply it.

There were notable exceptions even in the early days. Some authors such as Jan Mark and Robert Westall risked empowering their protagonists as anti-heroes, and ventured to play out the devastating imaginative consequences of traditional concepts of heroism in dystopian scenarios. Once this path has been taken, they argue, the only conceivable alternative is destructive or self-destructive violence. *The Ennead* (Mark, 1978) and *Futuretrack 5* (Westall, 1983) present more challenging and pessimistic visions of the human species than was customary in writing for the young at the time. Rather than adapting the classic dystopia, Mark and Westall embraced it fully, pushing back the boundaries of the juvenile text. Their writing started to imply an older teenage or young adult audience, which was predicted to be more mature, more intellectually confident and more accomplished at decoding texts than the hitherto fairly straightforward narratives had generally implied. The political intelligence and uncompromising imaginative coherence of these books was considerably heightened as a result, but their darker work, like that of the ground-breaking Robert Cormier, met with a very mixed critical reception.

Youth as a sacrifice: toxic future settings of the 1980s

So far I have outlined some of the narrative dilemmas authors have encountered when adapting the dystopia for young readers. These were to escalate significantly with the advent of a spate of texts which emerged in the 1980s in the wake of the precarious moments during the Cold War, when the world felt itself inch towards nuclear Armageddon. The genre suddenly depicted the dire implications of the bomb, in all its horror.

It seemed that children's novelists who decided to use the worst-case scenario felt compelled to signal the incontrovertible horror of this unthinkable future from the very outset. Thus it was common to find books such as *Brother in the Land* (Swindells, 1984), *The Last Children of Schevenborn* (Pausewang, 1988), *Wolf of Shadows* (Streiber, 1986) and *Children of the Dust* (Lawrence, 1985) that all concentrate initially upon the physical suffering of the victims of the blast (often innocent, powerless children) in lurid and horrifying detail. However, here, too, despite depicting the literal death of childhood, authors commonly displayed a reluctance to close down all hope by focusing ultimately on the teenage protagonist as a symbol of change: Danny and his girlfriend do not die, but leave to start afresh at the end of *Brother in the Land*; Roland in *The Last Children* turns to educating the children for peace; and *Children of the Dust* uses the metaphor of the mutant to imagine the evolution of a more highly evolved human species that may rise above the moral shortcomings of *Homo sapiens*. In the worst-case scenario of nuclear winter, though, authors found it undeniably difficult to sustain hope amidst the ruins without contradicting their underlying message that this devastated world must never be permitted to come to pass. Thus the narrative emphasis on tragedy in the dystopia, which is needed to carry the ideological warning, again posed immense tactical dilemmas for children's writers (see Sambell, 2003).

The contemporary scene: technology and youth as complex contested sites

I will now consider the ways in which during the past decade most futuristic fiction for the young has begun to experiment with a markedly more diverse range of narrative tactics, addressing a new range of themes which move well beyond the classic dystopia.

For a start, things that one generation regarded as futuristic possibility have already become reality for the next. The science fiction tropes of cloning, genetic engineering, neuropharmacology, virtual reality and hyper-reality, for instance, have already become lived experiences. The pace of technological change is accelerating dramatically in everyday domestic situations, as well as at a global level. Children and young people seem to be immersed in information technology and digital culture in ways their parents could scarcely imagine, still less comprehend. They use it for entertainment, schooling and communications, and while many adults flounder to keep up, youngsters are seen to embrace new interactive technologies (web technologies such as blogs, wikis, My Space, Bebo and You Tube, and entertainment devices like X-Box, Playstation and Wii) almost as naturally as breathing. There is a growing sense, then, that the future has already arrived and young people inhabit a radically different world.

In response, authors began to use futuristic fictional time to focus imaginative attention on the increasingly complex contested site between technology and youth. From the late 1990s radical new assemblages of youth, biology and technology became prominent in futuristic writing for young readers, with science fiction bioengineering tropes – the clone, the mutant and the cyborg, for instance – opening up exciting and terrifying new imaginative and narrative possibilities for young protagonists. In what follows I will highlight the ways in which this genre, and its new representations of children and young people, illuminates some key questions about literacy, literature and their relationship to contemporary young readers.

In *The Future of Childhood,* Alan Prout (2005) discusses the emergence of a dominant theoretical discourse which asserts that the very nature of childhood is altering as a result of technological change. Views of this change, he argues, are starkly divided. Some 'cyber-critics' such as Postman (1983) and Winn (1984) regard it as a crisis, feeling that digital media and the information explosion are not merely corrupting the young but are breaking down the distinction between children and adults such that the whole institution of childhood is 'disappearing'. This is assumed to be detrimental, based on assumptions that children and young people need, for their own good, to be maintained in a state of cultural dependence in relation to adults, who are assumed to be benign. In this paradigm the child is essentialized as an innocent other, whose 'loss' is then mourned. Technology, which is wrongly assumed to be a unitary phenomenon, is damned. On the other hand, Prout suggests, cyber-utopians like Katz (1997) assign contemporary digital technologies a positive value and children are hailed as the newly competent *avant-garde* of a new set of historical possibilities. Here the breakdown of the binary distinction between childhood and adulthood is welcomed and embraced. Prout asserts that these extreme positions have become politicized, so the more complex ground between them is often obscured.

I think it is possible to identify sharp contrasts between the simplistic stances adopted by some social theorists and the complexity and subtlety of futuristic fiction for young readers, which I believe is actively opening up new ways of representing young people and technology. Prout suggests that this is a vital enterprise, arguing that challenging and versatile new representations must be identified if current understandings and theories of childhood and youth are to develop. Under the pressure of a rapid sense of disintegration and breakdown, he suggests, traditional ways of representing the child are simply no longer adequate. Furthermore, unless theoretical understandings of young people can move forward, policy and practice for working for or with them will be restricted.

In my view a study of the genre has much to offer here, as the new representations of youth we see in futuristic fiction differ greatly from the innocent and dependent creatures of Postman's traditionalist vision. For instance, these books do not ignore the fact that the adult world continues to evidence a very mixed track record in terms of exerting a benign influence on its young. As futuristic fiction evolves, its strong dystopian undercurrent persists, designed to prompt searching questions about adult power in relation to children. In experimenting within the genre, authors do not evade the possibility of dire consequences and continue to warn that technology might be systematically used to manipulate, manufacture or even eradicate young identities.

Like their literary predecessors, youthful characters are still envisaged in many texts as victims of shocking abuse and experimentation. If anything, the genre has become tougher and more provocative. However, the ample graphic violence is never gratuitous. Nancy Farmer's *House of the Scorpion* (2002), for example, horrifyingly explores the perspective of the clone Matt, whose young body is viewed as a commodity that can be manipulated and exploited, his heart harvested as a spare part to lengthen the life of a rich old man. In Garth Nix's (1997) *Shades' Children*, each child is murdered at the age of 14, when his or her body is used to manufacture a killing machine to be used as a pawn in a life-or-death war game, remotely controlled by the Overlords. In a horrifyingly sickening episode, one of the creatures displays his remnant child consciousness while being vivisected by Shade. In Melvin Burgess's *Bloodtide* (1999) and *Bloodsong* (2007), children are cloned, 'brewed' and modified by their parents in a brutal future world of eugenics and ethnic cleansing. In James Patterson's *Maximum Ride* trilogy (2006, 2007, 2008), children are stolen by a company, ITEX, that biologically modifies them into 'mutant freaks' that are later sold as weapons. ITEX seeks to create a perfect world, free of disease and poverty, by wiping out huge swathes of the population. The dystopian elements are clearly foregrounded and no punches are pulled.

However, on another level, all these authors experiment with new ways of imagining young people, seeing them simultaneously as an evolved species that is changed and empowered and as one that is exploited and manipulated. For instance, Nix's (1997) teenage protagonists possess 'change talents' which enable them to exert some capacity to challenge and ultimately overthrow the damaging adult world. Burgess's Sigurd is, like Schwarzenegger's Terminator, a post-human biotechnological being who is powerfully enhanced and utterly indestructible (Burgess, 2005). Johnny Online in *Hybrids* (Thorpe, 2007) and Fang in *Maximum Ride: Saving the World and Other Extreme Sports* (Patterson, 2007) both use blogging, and new forms of digital communication, to raise awareness and incite rebellion. Max and her 'mutant bird-kids', the Flock, are cast as powerfully evolved beings who successfully fight to save the world (Patterson, 2006, 2007, 2008).

Such narrative devices are not being used as evasive imaginative solutions which simply avoid or circumvent the dire consequences of dystopian projections. Indeed, many of these novels do not end happily – if anything, the tendency to depict the defeat of the young protagonist is carried through more forcefully than used to be generally accepted. Sigurd, for instance, expires 'in a mist of blood', and two of Shade's children, Drum and Ninde, knowingly perish to protect and save their alternative teenage family group. I think that what we are seeing here are complex, richly ambiguous representations and negotiations of the relationships between young people and technologies which begin to challenge and redefine assumptions about the future of youth and child/adult politics.

In other words, these representations of young characters, who embody new socio-technical assemblages, do not act as simple prophecies or as unambiguous warnings, but as richly ambiguous representations designed to prompt important questions and explorations. As Prout argues, the effects of new technologies will not fold into childhood in a simple or uncontested way, and we must explore a whole network of complex connections if we are to grasp the process. In this way futuristic texts for young readers are beginning to 'offer instances of the assemblages of culture and nature, of body and technology, of discourse and materiality to which those studying childhood must pay attention if we are even to begin to understand the trajectories childhood will take' (Prout, 2005, 141).

Assumptions about the changing nature of a young readership

The unlocking of experimental narrative possibilities I am highlighting here could be regarded as going hand in hand with a growing authorial confidence in the implied reader of futuristic fiction as a youth or young adult, rather than a child, again blurring the boundaries between children and adults. Judging from the complexity and ugly brutality of the fictions now being produced, young readers are seen by authors to be more capable of appreciating complex ethical and global issues, more aware of the world, and more resilient than their predecessors. They are being addressed as more politically literate, less idealistic and less naïve readers. They are also, interestingly, being seen as more sophisticated interpreters of texts.

Innovative authors such as Nix and Burgess are beginning to rework and update futuristic fiction for youth, consciously echoing the virtual realities and diverse narrative formats with which many young readers are likely to be familiar from their experience with a diverse range of media and information and communication technologies. It is important to note that the form, not simply the content, of the literature these writers produce is becoming increasingly hybridized. A complex blend of science fiction, dystopia, romance and horror is emerging. Burgess even adds Norse saga and romance to his mix.

This parallels the ways in which popular culture has become increasingly hybridized, with dystopias being blended with horror and science fiction and mainstreamed in such films, TV shows and games as *Bladerunner, Terminator, Alien, Minority Report, Resident Evil, Doom, Buffy* and *The Matrix*. Young people are often familiar with these diverse media narratives and authors are starting to draw upon their conventions, which then inform and expand the literary genre. For instance, both Burgess's and Nix's works plunge the reader into a fictional world which simulates a violent 'shoot-'em-up' computer game. Sigurd, on one level, is like an avatar, whose player has downloaded health 'cheats', so that when he 'dies' horribly he is resurrected, being made to play the game relentlessly, however bloody and dark it may become (Burgess, 2005). Such strategies afford the readership knowingness, insider status and the allusive, inter-textual cultural capital of non-literary media forms that are immensely popular with young people.

I think it especially interesting that Burgess presupposes that this will heighten, rather than reduce, young readers' capacity to engage with his complex literary work. His young readers, judging by their reviews, agree, frequently commenting on the potential his futuristic books have for transferring into other media. This highlights the ways in which writers are using media convergence within the genre to negotiate and question not just changing views of childhood, youth and adulthood, but also the changing nature of literacy itself. It is as if many skilled authors are actively changing the form of their futuristic stories, not simply the content, to appeal to young readers, particularly boys, who are perceived as skilled, 'differently literate' (Millard, 1997) and competent interpreters of texts – albeit, perhaps, non-canonical texts. This flies in the face of the plethora of accounts of crisis that surround young people, which, as Gibson (2007) and Pullman (1993) both argue, habitually frame young males as 'reluctant readers' or dismiss their preferred media texts (such as comics or games), often misguidedly, as simple and unchallenging narratives, or even as direct threats to literacy. Instead a counter-argument is perhaps emerging in futuristic fiction, in which young people are posited as more competent readers and social actors; they have grown up experiencing the hybridity of complex narrative media, in which computers and games appear animated, with a life and intelligence of their own.

Bloodsong (Burgess, 2007) is one of the most exciting and innovative futuristic texts I have read to date, insofar as it unlocks startlingly new representations of the male teenage protagonist. The 15-year-old Sigurd is not simply a Romantic other to be protected: Burgess represents him instead as both victim and victor, with an intense emotional range, awareness and moral complexity. Moreover, Burgess's futuristic work posits an intelligent, sensitive (male?) teenage reader, not a dangerously aggressive or easily led one. He achieves this by interrogating, rather than ignoring or condemning, the causes and effects of the all-too-authentic pressures of teenage risk-taking and thrill-seeking. Above all, Burgess seeks to speak to young readers in their own idiom, by privileging and acknowledging popular forms of narrative which they habitually consume – not because he has a view of a reader who needs rescuing, but because of a view of the contemporary teenager as a changed type of reader, skilled with varying narrative forms and used to manipulating multiple narrative realities.

Conclusion

This futuristic fiction is a far cry from the didacticism we saw earlier in the chapter because, paradoxically, it works quite conventionally. In Burgess's own words, it is literature, not a lesson:

> Once you have decided that young people can contextualise narrative in their own right, make a moral judgment on it in their own right, recognize the difference between story and real life in their own right and understand how it relates to their own lives in many more ways than example or advice, you can let go of any attempt to lecture them, help them or, worst of all, educate them, and simply tell your story. (2004, 294)

Bibliography

Alberghene, J. (1988) Childhood's End?, *Children's Literature in Education*, **13**, 188–93.

Browne, T. (1980) *Red Zone*, MacMillan Topliner.

Burgess, M. (1999) *Bloodtide*, Andersen Press.

Burgess, M. (2004) Sympathy for the Devil, *Children's Literature in Education*, **35** (4), 289-300.

Burgess, M. (2007) *Bloodsong*, Penguin Books Ltd.

Christopher, J. (1970) *The Guardians*, Hamish Hamilton.

Crew, H. (2004) Not So Brave a World: The representation of human cloning in science fiction for young adults, *Lion and Unicorn,* **28** (2), 203-21.

Eakin, M. (1973) The Changing World of Science and the Social Sciences. In Haviand, V. (ed.), *Children's Literature: views and reviews*, Bodley Head.

Egoff, S. (1969) Pleasures and Precepts: changing emphases in the writing and criticism of children's literature. In Egoff, S., Stubbs, G. T. and Ashley, L. F. (eds), *Only Connect: reading and children's literature*, Oxford University Press.

Engdahl, S. (1980) Perspective on the Future: the quest of space age young people. In Lenz, M. and Mahood, R. (eds), *Young Adult Literature: background and criticism*, American Library Association.

Farmer, N. (2002) *The House of the Scorpion*, Atheneum Books.

Frankel, B. (1987) *The Post-Industrial Utopians*, Polity Press.

Gibson, M. (2007) *Graphic Novels Across the Curriculum*, www.ltscotland.org.uk/literacy/findresources/graphicnovels/section/intro.asp [accessed 7 June 2007].

Harrison, B. (1987) Howl Like the Wolves, *Children's Literature in Education*, **15**, 86.

Hoover, H. M. (1973) *Children of Morrow*, Four Winds Press.

Hoover, H. M. (1980) *This Time of Darkness*, Viking Press.

Hughes, M. (1978) *The Tomorrow City*, Hamish Hamilton.

Hughes, M. (1984) *Devil on My Back*, Atheneum.

Huxley, A. (1932) Brave New World, Chatto & Windus.

Katz, J. (1997) *The Digital Citizen*, **5** (12), (December), 68-82, 274-5.

Kesteven, G. R. (1977) *The Awakening Water*, Chatto.

Lawrence, L. (1985) *Children of the Dust*, Bodley Head.

Mark, J. (1978) *The Ennead*, Kestrel Books.

Millard, E. (1997). *Differently Literate: boys, girls and the schooling of literacy*, Routledge Falmer.

Nix, G. (1997) *Shade's Children*, HarperCollins.

Orwell, G. (1949) *Nineteen Eighty-four*, Secker & Warburg.

Patterson, J. (2006) *Maximum Ride: The Angel Experiment*, Time Warner Book Group.

Patterson, J. (2007) *Maximum Ride: Saving the World and Other Extreme Sports*, Time Warner Book Group.

Patterson, J. (2008) *Maximum Ride: The Final Warning*, Little, Brown & Co.

Pausewang, G. (1988) *The Last Children of Schevenborn*, Douglas and MacIntyre Ltd.

Plotz, J. (1988) The Disappearance of Childhood: parent–child role reversals

Postman, N. (1983) *The Disappearance of Childhood*, W. H. Allen.

Prout, A. (2005) *The Future of Childhood*, Routledge Falmer.

Pullman, P. (1993) In Barker, K. (ed.), *Graphic Account: the selection and promotion of graphic novels in libraries for young people*, Library Association Publishing.

Richemont, E. (1990) *The Game*, Walker.

Sambell, K. (2003) Presenting the Case for Social Change: the creative dilemma of dystopian writing for children. In Hintz, C. and Ostry, E. (eds), *Utopian and Dystopian Writing for Children and Young Adults*, Routledge, 163–78.

Schlee, A. (1979) *The Vandal*, Macmillan.

Scutter, H. (1996) Representing the Child: postmodern versions of Peter Pan. In Bradford, C. (ed.), *Writing the Australian Child*, University of WA Press and Deakin University, Nedlands, Western Australia, 1–16.

Steele, M. (1973) Realism, Truth and Honesty. In Haviland, V. (ed.), *Children's Literature: views and reviews*, Bodley Head.

Stephens, J. (1992) Post-Disaster Fiction: the problematics of a genre, *Papers*, **3** (3), 126–30.

Streiber, W. (1986) *Wolf of Shadows*, Hodder and Stoughton.

Swindells, R. (1984) *Brother in the Land*, Oxford University Press.

Swindells, R. (1990) *Daz 4 Zoe*, Hamish Hamilton.

Thorpe, D. (2007) *Hybrids*, Harper Collins.

Townsend, J. R. (1971) *A Sense of Story*, Longman.

Townsend, J. R. (1980) *King Creature Come*, Oxford University Press.

Tully, J. (1984) *Natfact 7*, Methuen.

Prince, A. (1986) *The Others*, Methuen.

Westall, R. (1979) The Vacuum and the Myth. In Kennerley, P. (ed), *Teenage Reading*, Ward Lock.

Westall, R. (1983) *Futuretrack 5*, Kestrel

Winn, M. (1984) *Children Without Childhood*, Penguin.

Chapter 8

Cheers Ta: reflections on making poetry accessible to all

MIKE GARRY

Editors' preface

Mike's background in library and information work, particularly his experience in working with young people, gives him a distinct perspective on bringing literature to readers. In this chapter he uses his work with a variety of groups in society to illustrate how one can make poetry fun, exciting and a part of everyday life.

While maintaining the theme of works of imagination, Mike takes a very different approach to the other authors in this section. He is concerned with enthusing people from children to pensioners to read, listen to, write and perform poetry. His use of diary entries is a novel way of illustrating the way in which, as a poet, he develops a relationship with his audience. This can be adapted and adopted by library and information professionals and incorporated in any reader development scheme.

Introduction

I believe the most appropriate way to tell someone how I bring literature to readers is to tear a month out of my diary and go through it, to show the many different ways in which I, as a writer, poet, a publisher and educationalist, promote reading and writing. I have chosen a fairly representative month: June 2007.

Think about it
I don't want to think about
These things that I've been thinking about
Cos when I think about
The things I think about
I think
Don't think about them
Think about something else
Think about something that won't
Make you think about
The things that I've been thinking about
Think about it

Taken from Garry, M. (2007) *Mancunian Meander*, Cheers Ta

A little about the poet
A poet?

I hate it when people ask me what I do for a living because it takes at least 20 minutes to explain fully. What I tell people when they do ask usually depends upon how much time I have and whether they are asking me out of politeness or whether they genuinely want to know.

If I tell them, with my strong Mancunian accent, that I write poetry, they usually say things like: 'What, you make pottery?'

Then I reply with, 'No, I write and perform poetry', putting extra emphasis on the word 'p-o-e-t-r-y'.

Then they reply with: 'Ooh right – I've never met a real poet before. Do you live in the Lake District? Have you got a frilly shirt? Do you like flowers?'

If I tell them what I studied at university and what I feel is my 'trade', I tell them I'm a librarian. And the reply is: 'A librarian. Do you have to go to university to become a librarian? What do you study all day, how to stamp books?'

To which I reply: 'I buy the books you read and generally learn how to organize knowledge.'

If I tell people I am a publisher, I get the weirdest of looks. Some people think I'm really rich and others seem to think I peddle porn.

In all three cases, I'm in a lose–lose situation.

How I work

When I was approached by the editors to write a chapter for this book, I had a similar dilemma to the one I have when people ask me what I do for a living. I had to ask myself, how do I attempt to bring literature to readers?

The answer I came up with was that I bring literature to readers in many different ways: through live performance, through workshops, through publishing and through school visits.

But I still didn't think this told the full story (excuse the pun).

How I got to here

Reading is important to me and has been from a very early age because it provided me with the quickest and easiest form of escape. I went to the café with Sophie in *The Tiger Who Came to Tea*, I lived in a peach with James, I sat on the wall with Humpty, I did hand-clap rhymes and skipping games and knew all the words to songs by Sweet and Slade because the reality of growing up in a 1970s inner-city council housing estate in Manchester was not as beautiful as it appears in the black and white photographs my mother still keeps in a large biscuit tin in her pantry.

A good catholic education provided me with a staple poetic diet: mesmerizing stories by Roald Dahl and tales of Finn McCool sat on the carpet with Miss McCoomb in a Moss Side primary school. There were lashings of rhyme and repetition from mass, stations of the cross and benediction, and I was lured into language by the beauty of words like genuflection, Golgotha and Gethsemane.

I grew up in an Irish household with a large extended family of musicians and storytellers. I loved language, rhythm, rhyme and the musicality of the voice. The entourage of drunken singers, musicians and poets my father picked up and brought home from the pub provided great entertainment and education for my young ear. My future role as a poet and wordsmith was clearly mapped out at quite an early age.

Slowly but surely I found my voice through reading, writing and listening. I hated any form of violence and fighting, and learned quite quickly that fights could be avoided if you could talk your way out of them, or publicly ridiculed the aggressor so much that he'd walk away with his head hung in shame.

My first Saturday job was at a clothes shop called Stolen from Ivor where I worked with Johnny Marr of the Smiths. I later shared poems and lyrics with Morrissey. As a teenager I hung out at Anthony Wilson's Hacienda surrounded by the mournful Joy Division, Paul Morley and the reckless Bez and Shaun Ryder. I was drawn to creative people, especially those who were creative with words.

I worked in a public library for 13 years, organizing reading promotions and literary events – not for the fun of it, but because it was important to me and to lots of other people. For many young people, literature is the way out – not TV shows like the 'X Factor'.

I try to write for an hour a day. Sometimes this might turn into two or three hours – it is unpredictable. Equally important is the fact that I read work by other poets. The 'poet' that claims not to read any other poets is not a poet but a pretender.

I'll choose a poet whose name I like or who has been recommended to me, and I will read around them for a month and build up my knowledge of them as a writer and a person. I never studied literature at university so I think this is important.

I have attended the Arvon Foundation in Hebden Bridge and studied poetry under the tutelage of Henry Normal, Simon Armitage, Graham Mort and Peter and Ann Sansom. I am constantly learning from other poets, writers and the students I work with.

My diary: June 2007
Friday 1 June 2007

I do a poetry workshop for Salford City Council in Lucy Winskill House in Irlam with a group of 20 pensioners.

I do a two-hour session that involves me introducing a poet to them. This week it was Seamus Heaney. I love Heaney and had the honour of meeting him briefly at the Hay-on-Wye literature festival in 2006. We look at three of his poems during the session and I discover that the majority of people attending are 70-plus and can recite a full poem they know off by heart.

I always try to involve some writing so we do some haiku and finish the session with a read-around.

These people are an honour to work with: engaged, engaging, interested and interesting. They inspire me to live to 100 and they all go home wanting to read more.

Saturday 2 June 2007

I've been commissioned by Salford City Council to produce a poem that celebrates a piece of public art that has been created in Eccles. The artwork is a celebration of two industries, steel and margarine, which were massive employers in the area until 1979. It depicts a couple dancing a tango and is to be placed on a roundabout, so that when you drive past the couple appear to be rotating. I want to write a piece that complements the dancers, so I have chosen to write it in the form of a *rondeau redoublé*.

A *rondeau redoublé* is not an easy form to write: it uses only two rhymes throughout, repeats whole lines and has an awkward repeated half-line at the end. However, its cyclical nature will tie in perfectly with the piece of public art.

I spend the day looking at different examples of the *rondeau redoublé* and trying to write one. I love my job.

Sunday 3 June 2007

Sunday is always prep day for me. I'm sitting down with my diary and looking at what I have to do for the week and if anything specific needs preparing. This usually means hunting down some obscure poem or poet or typing up the poems of people I've worked with in the previous week.

Monday 4 June 2007

I work with Brownhill School in Rochdale. It is an SEBD (Social, Emotional and Behavioural Difficulties) secondary school where the kids have done very little English as part of their education, so myself, Sherry Ashworth and Melvin Burgess have been brought in to get a magazine together that involves stories, poems, riddles, reviews and interviews done by the kids.

Over the course of the day I work with 15 very troubled young people. I show them appropriate poems and short stories that I think they will like – *Chivvy* by Michael Rosen, *Yes* by Adrian Mitchell and some poems from my second book, *Mancunian Meander* – and try to get the idea across to them that writing something down is not a 'girly' thing to do and can help us arrange our thoughts.

I have a really good relationship with some of these kids, and once barriers are broken down they will write. I encourage all the kids I work with to join the library and to use it. I sometimes build this into the project, whereby we will visit the library, meet the librarian and have a behind-the-scenes tour.

In the afternoon I go into the Summerhouse studio in Manchester. I'm really fortunate that I've got a group of close fiends who have a wonderful top floor studio in the heart of Manchester's Northern Quarter where I've got a desk and a computer and people around me who care about what I do. I work with Anthony Ball, the head of Ant Ball Design and a top designer, to put the work the young people did in the morning into a magazine that we hope to pull together by the end of the project.

Tuesday 5 June 2007

I work with teachers and provide INSET (In-service Education & Training) to schools. As a librarian I helped set up a network of homework centres across Manchester, and worked closely with school-aged boys trying to encourage them to read. I discovered just how difficult this was but learned certain techniques that worked. I think it is important to cascade any ideas I have to parents, teachers and youth workers that can help others get young people to read.

Today's INSET session is called *Boys Don't Cry (or read and write)*, and I run through a range of ideas I have that get lads to pick up newspapers, magazines and eventually books. I work with 20 teachers from across Bury Bolton and Rochdale for an afternoon, sharing my ideas.

Wednesday 6 June 2007

I wrote this late last night:

Clock this

12 naughty 13-year-old schoolboys
14 miles from 15 even naughtier 16-year-old schoolgirls
All reading Just 17.
Cruising towards each other in an 18 seater mini bus
Travelling north and south respectively along the A19
The boys drink fizzy pop and burp loudly and laugh
The girls sip warm bottled water through a straw
Some 20 minutes later having travelled 21 miles
A 22 tonne truck travelling 23 miles above the speed limit
Skids
Twists
Jack knives and flips
Producing 24 bloody casualties

Clock this
1 hour later 2 people kiss in the doorway of a 3 bed roomed
Terraced home in fallow field Manchester
He's been away for 4 nights and missed his wife and 5 daughters
so much
He swears he'll never leave those girls again
Then, a 6-sense twitch in mid kiss
Something a miss
7 letters later
He asks of his eldest daughter
8 hours away
Skiing in Scotland on a school trip
She'll ring tonight at 9 his wife insists
The ten o'clock local news reports of the truck and the handful of
survivors
Seconds later the phone rings
'Yes Elle.
A mole on her left cheek.
Yes.
Year 11.'
He replaces the receiver and wishes he was 12.

It's a bit messy but I'll tidy it up later.

I do a lot of work for the Rochdale Education and Learning (REAL) Trust and Rochdale's EIC (Excellence in Cities). They bring artists into schools to work with groups of young people. They have asked me to work in Woodlands, a newly formed school with two Year-6 classes and to compile an anthology of their work.

I work with 30 pupils in the morning and 32 in the afternoon. I introduce them to a range of poetic styles including haiku, tanka, kennings and riddles and generally have fun with literature and instil the idea that our book will be produced and designed by the children with my assistance. After showing them the poetic techniques and some examples, I get them to write themselves. I encourage them to edit their own work, share it with their friends and family and then, when they are happy with the poems, they'll read them out in class.

I think it's important for young people to read their work out loud. They

love to perform and if reading their poems aloud allows them to do that
– great – their confidence will grow the more they do it.

Ultimately my priority must be to have fun and from having fun the pupils
will learn. So I turn the classroom upside down. I stand at the back of the
class and get them to turn around in an effort to get them to look at things
from a different perspective. I get them to read aloud to the group. I share
my favourite poems with them and generally have great fun playing with
words and poems.

Thursday 7 June 2007

I spend all day in the Summerhouse studio with my designer working on
the Brownhill magazine and Woodlands anthology. In the past five years
I have produced ten anthologies of young people's poetry. I think it is
important for young people to see their work in print in a well-designed
book. I always involve them in design and artwork, and try to achieve a 'look
and feel' that will encourage other young people to pick the book up.

Friday 8 June 2007

I continue to work at the Summerhouse studio with the designer on the
Brownhill magazine and Woodlands anthology.

In the afternoon I meet with an officer from the URBIS museum in
Manchester who has asked me to compere and host the '0161' live summer
music art and literature festival in Cathedral Gardens.

I am regularly asked to host and present live events and to support live
bands. I enjoy doing poems to a non-poetry audience because they never
expect it to be any good, so they are shocked when they hear poems they
like. If I had £1 for every time someone came up to me after a gig and said,
'I've never heard performance poetry before and that was brilliant', I'd have
enough to pay my latest tax bill.

Saturday 9 June 2007

Day off.

Sunday 10 June 2007

Prep day and I spend some time writing a monologue for the Manchester
Monologues competition. I don't go in much for competitions, but I like the
theme and the prize is to perform it at the opening of the Hacienda Exhibition

at URBIS in July and to be published in a collection of Manchester Monologues.

I listen to Lemn Sissay on Radio 4 doing a programme about travelling by train. Lemn is a top international poet and has supported me throughout my career. I've watched him grow as a poet from performing as an 18-year-old at the Green Room in Manchester to having his own one-man show, Something Dark, at the Battersea Arts Centre in London. I text him after the programme and he phones me back to thank me for my comments and we arrange to meet next time I'm down in London.

Monday 11 June 2007

Distribution day. As a small publisher I distribute books to various bookshops throughout the north west. I spent the day travelling to branches of Waterstones, Borders and Foyle's, and to local independent bookshops, providing more stock and seeing how stock is selling. I always try to get to know the manager and talk to him or her about my stock. They will then make an effort to sell the book by putting copies in 'face on' displays at eye level. Every bookshop manager I have ever met is passionate about literature and if they find something they like they'll shout about it.

I talk to frontline store staff and give them signed copies of my book, put them on guest lists for my gigs and ask them to recommend my books to readers.

Tuesday 12 June 2007

Back at Brownhill SEBD school where they have an Ofsted inspection. I work with the 'I Can' group and show them how a found poem can be created from old newspapers and magazines with a pair of scissors and some glue. We cut out lots of poetic headlines and put them together in an order that creates a poem, as the Beatles did with 'A Day in a Life' and 'I am the Walrus'. They love it and have great fun throughout the session, and I get a glowing report from Ofsted so everyone wins.

Wednesday 13 June 2007

Meeting with Apples and Snakes co-ordinator for the 'Inside Out' project. Apples and Snakes 'stretches the boundary of poetry in education and performance. We aim to give a voice to challenging, diverse and dynamic poets and encourage the appreciation of poetry by all'. I work in prisons with young offenders getting them to read, write and perform poems. I did a three-month residency at Hindley Prison and we are planning to do another residency at Thorn Cross in Warrington. I am also publishing a collection of poems written by women prisoners at Styal Prison. Today the co-ordinator and myself were proofreading the final mock-up before it goes off to the printer. I find myself constantly changing heads like Worzxel Gummidge – one minute poetry head, the next publisher head, etc.

Thursday 14 June 2007

I am booked to present prizes at the Bolton Literacy Trust presentation evening. I worked with a range of youth groups in schools, colleges and youth clubs, encouraging young people to get involved in a poetry competition on the theme of Identity. The project was a great success. Today I do a reading, talk about my role as a poet and present prizes to the winning poets.

Friday 15 June 2007

During the punk era of the late 1970s, many bands would have a poet as support before the main act. John Cooper Clarke was famous for it and was known as a punk poet. I had the honour to meet John when I performed at the Cohesion Festival in Manchester in 2006. I signed a copy of *Mancunian Meander* and went to give it to him. To my amazement he said he had a copy already and that the Radio 1 DJ Mark Radcliffe had recommended it. He then said, 'It's gritty stuff.'

I was honoured.

I've been asked to provide support for a wonderful band called 'I Am Kloot' in Blackburn, and 300 people cram into a club/bar to hear me perform for 20 minutes before the band and sell books after the gig, and I get lots of people asking for details and website information so that they can buy books from there.

I've known Johnny Bramwell (lead singer of I Am Kloot) for 20 years and watched him grow from a singer/songwriter from Hyde to what he is now – an international artist. Kloot are massive in Europe and have been asked by the director Jimmy Boyle to do the title track for his latest film 'Sunshine'. They are one of my favourite bands, so to be asked to support them is a very special honour for me.

The last time I was in Blackburn I did a great gig for the library service. As I was leaving the club I'd just performed in I noticed that the library was right next door.

Excursions on a wobbly rail

I am Laurel
You are Hardy
I'm not daft
You're not barmy
I hope my son will join the army
I hope my daughter will become a sorter
In a sock factory in Hyde
In a sock factory in Hyde
I am Morecambe
You are wise
Have you ever noticed the shape of a cyclist's thighs?
Yanks don't call chips Chips
They call them fries
Let's go once more under the bridge that my dad built single-handed
These excursions on a wobbly rail are becoming far too candid
I'll be Lee Majors in the Six Million Dollar Man
If you're Chuck Connors in Branded – If you're Chuck Connors in
Branded.

Saturday 16 and Sunday 17 2007

My work is very intense and I work with diverse challenging groups, so sometimes I need a break. I just read and write for much of the weekend and try very hard not to think about work (see 'Think About It' poem) – but if you love what you do it is difficult to stop. In a sense I am my work, I am very passionate about it – I live and breathe it.

Monday 18 June 2007

I work with another group of 70-plus in a place called Caddishead in Salford. This group is different, not as close-knit as the group in Irlam so things don't work as well and I only work with four people. Sometimes things don't work – it is beyond your control. I used to take things personally and blame myself. However, the more experienced I have become, the more I realize and accept that owing to reasons beyond your control things won't always work.

In the evening I work for Apples and Snakes on the 'Inside Out' project. I work in a children's home in Manchester. This is one of my favourite jobs.

I work with eight looked-after children in a wonderful home with passionate and caring staff.

I do a lot of work with looked-after children throughout the UK and this 'home' is a template for how they should all be run. Don't get me wrong, the kids are still challenging and have loads of problems, but they are great writers and people.

I work with the teenage writer Melvin Burgess. He's a mate of mine and he is writing a book about kids in care and wanted to come in with me to get a feeling for the care system – it's great because it encourages the young people to read his books as well and he's quite handy at splitting up fighting kids.

Tuesday 19 June 2007

Back to brilliant Brownhill to work with a young man called Kieran who is the Billy Casper of the 21st century – he is a brilliant writer who has lots of problems with violence and anger, but when he gets into the countryside and watches birds or plays in the woods he is always calmer and violence and anger are not an issue. He wrote this over the weekend:

Trouble free

The Hills keep me from trouble
Watching Hollingworth Lake from above
Watching the boats
Then playing in Birchill woods
Or great Howarth where the deer roam wild – untroubled
Me Jordan and lewis
Free
Chilled and calm
No hypos
No alarm
Swimming in the river Roach near Heywood
Rafting on a lilo
Catching fish – filleting – then feasting on them for tea
Tony or Ian Riding me on the handle bars or saddle seat
Camping by the river
Learning the names of birds and the sound of water
Bringing peace to my mind

Me Jordan and Lewis
Me Tony and Ian
Free
Chilled and calm
No hypos
No alarm
Kieran

When I read things like this I realize that I have got the best job in the world.

Wednesday 20 July 2007

Back to Woodlands primary school for my final weekly visit. I have worked with them for four weeks now and today is the final writing session. I do some Benjamin Zephaniah with the children. I have worked with Benjamin in Manchester Art Gallery on an image and identity project and admire his work and politics.

The aim of this project was to work with the children for four weeks and produce an anthology of their work. They have really motivated teachers who like the stuff we have done, so the kids' work is good. By the end of the day I give them a deadline of Monday to have everything together for publication.

Thursday 21 June 2007

I work in the Summerhouse studio all day with a designer bringing together the Brownhill magazine and starting to get ideas together for the Woodlands anthology.

In the evening I have a meeting with the head of English at a secondary school in Rochdale who wants me to do a three-month residency as writer-in-residence at the school.

Friday 22 June 2007

I work in a secondary school in Sheffield looking at the 'poetry from other cultures' in the GCSE anthology.

At 3.30 I jump on a train to London's Islington Academy to support I Am Kloot.

Again, a brilliant gig – 300 people listening to the performance. Sometimes when I support bands it is difficult to get them quiet and sometimes it doesn't work. I remember at one point during my performance listening to the crowd and you could hear a pin drop.

A problem that I have is carrying books. I knew that I could have sold at least 100 books tonight but, because I was working in Sheffield during the day, I didn't want to be carrying boxes of books around with me. I try to carry round publicity materials that will direct people to my website at www.cheersta.co.uk.

My stuff seems to work really well with bands, so I'm starting to be asked to do festivals. The money is rubbish but it means bringing my poems to hundreds of people a day and I get to meet all my musical heroes.

Saturday 23 June 2007

I am due in Bolton Town Hall at 12 noon for the Bolton Book Awards. My train is cancelled from Euston so I spend some time in the British Library doing a bit of library geeky stuff and looking at some of the exhibitions.

Sunday 24 June 2007

Prep day and lots of reading and writing. Read the Sunday papers and wrote this:

Careworn
Bloated newsreaders report on lost children
Stolen by day devils posing as parents
Handing melting ice creams
To nobodies some bodies everything
Crying silently for Mum
And asking if they can go home now
'Can I go home now?'
The curtains are drawn in the sunless heat of daytime hotel rooms
Where cartoon network
And McDonald's Happy Meal boxes
Are the only memories of home
Home where Mum and Dad and the twins will never move from again
'Cos what if she phones?'

Monday 25 June 2007

I go to Woodlands school to pick up the finished poems and artwork for publication. I go for a second meeting with the head of English at the Rochdale secondary school, then race to Summerhouse with the poems and artwork and start to work on getting the anthology together with the designer.

Tuesday 26 June 2007

I meet with the Apples and Snakes co-ordinator to discuss the next stage of the Inside Out project.

I meet with my designer and we continue making books and magazines.

Wednesday 27 June 2007

I travel to Clitheroe to do some work with a range of classes in a secondary school and race back for a meeting with the arts officer from the Arts Council concerning the publication of a book by the brilliant poet Marvin Cheeseman and a new CD of work by a poet called Diké Omejé who tragically died in January 2007 of a cancer that he had carried for 18 years.

I published Diké's first book and I am working with the Commonword writers' group, the Manchester Literature Festival and the Arts Council to ensure that his name lives on.

Diké was an amazing poet and a brilliant friend. We shared so much together. We did our first performances on the same stage on the same night. We shared the same doctor. We both had terrible teeth and spent hours in dentists' chairs and swapped tales of drills, injections and root canal surgery. We shared a room at the Arvon Foundation. I was the last person he spoke to before he died. I miss him so much and not a day goes by that I don't think about him.

The world lost a wonderful poet and man on 12 January 2007.

Thursday 28 June 2007

I spend all day planning and writing a piece for an academic book for librarians.

I constantly question what I do. I do loads of work with children and young people and I love it and feel honoured to be able to spout my feeling about poetry and reading to large sections of the community – but I don't write a lot of kids' stuff. Manchester United and UNICEF are doing a book with libraries to raise funds and I have been asked to write a kids' poem for it – furthermore they have only given me 24 hours to do it. I've really struggled but, in the end, I've come up with this:

If you want to be a footballer

If you want to be a footballer make sure you brush your teeth
Be in bed at eight o'clock
Never cause your mother any grief
Be kind to people all the time
Don't drink beer
Don't drink wine
Don't smoke fags and you'll be fine
But always eat your greens
If you want to be a footballer
You must work hard at school
Visit the library everyday cos reading books is cool
Do our homework every night
Never argue
Never fight
Score the winner in the final with your eyes closed tight
But always eat your greens
If you want to be a footballer
Make sure you do your training
Even if your favourite programme's on
Even if it's raining
Clean your kit after every game
And don't wear boots just because of the name
Keep fit and healthy and you'll find fame
But ALWAYS
ALWAYS
ALWAYS
ALWAYS
Eat your greens

Friday 29 June 2007

I catch an early train to London to compete in the UK Slam Championships.

Slam is unique. It is a competitive form of performance poetry. It originated in Chicago and has now become a worldwide phenomenon. Eminem used it in his film *Eight Mile*. The audience give each performer a mark out of ten and the winner is the one with the most points.

It is a great event and really well organized by the Theatre Royal in

Stratford, east London. The semifinal has 20 poets, two judges from the audience and three specialist judges including someone from the Poetry Society, an actor and an established poet. Each competitor has two three-minute opportunities to perform a poem and get marked by judges.

The poets with the ten highest scores go through to the final which will be held on Saturday night. I got the highest marks and won the semifinal, which meant I go last in the final on Saturday night.

Saturday 30 June 2007

I stay with a friend and do a bit of prep for the final. It is good to sit down and have a bit of a practise; I don't get a lot of opportunities to do it.

I compete in the final with ten other poets from the length and breadth of the UK and come third. You can't take slams too seriously because the results are more to do with the mood of the audience than anything else. I had fun and spoke to a lot of people about my work and was booked to do some work for the Poetry Society in London in July as a result.

The conclusion of my tale

This wasn't a particularly busy month and I still brought literature to over 2000 people in one guise or another. I've done gigs, readings, workshops talks and training. I have travelled from Manchester to Yorkshire to London to Clitheroe and back again. Most importantly, I have enjoyed every minute of it and, hopefully, so have the people I have performed to, trained and published.

Section 4

Future directions

Introduction:
Section 4

This section examines changes that are taking place in the ways in which literature is brought to the reader. It considers a number of key developments and future scenarios that may impact on reader development. As such the chapters and their content are varied in scope and range.

First there is a detailed analysis of the development of e-books, followed by a review of the impact that alternative formats and distribution methods are having on the traditional book and its communities. The third chapter considers the challenges, opportunities and rewards facing the traditional owner-run bookshop today. A final chapter reflects upon the role of academics and practitioners in guaranteeing that issues and developments within the field of reader development are taught to future professionals.

Chapter 9

Premature elegies: e-books, electronic publishing and reading

CLAIRE WARWICK

Editors' preface

This chapter provides a detailed examination of the e-book, its marketplace and its readership and how these have developed over the past decade. The author considers the e-book and its history, the role of the reader, the technologies available and the users of e-books. In addition she discusses hypertext fiction, online bookselling and locating rare and second-hand texts. This chapter encourages the practitioner to consider adopting new strategies in order to meet the demands resulting from the availability of these new technologies.

Introduction

In the late 1990s publishers thought they had discovered an exciting new way of delivering literature to readers, and a promising new revenue stream: the e-book. The hype about e-books became pervasive, insisting that we would soon be reading almost everything online, from academic journals to glossy magazines – and yet, around ten years later, paper is still the dominant medium for most types of publication, and certainly for literature, and the number of books and magazines published is greater than ever. Literature is largely delivered to readers on paper, in the form of traditional print on paper. So what happened to all the overheated predictions about the future, and has anything really changed as a result of electronic publishing? This chapter will examine not only e-books, but also the effects that electronic delivery of information of various sorts have had on the way that publishers and authors deliver literature to readers.

The e-book and its history

The definition of an e-book is inseparable from the history of hype, bust and cautious retrenchment that has characterized the e-book. To use a broad definition, it is simply a digital version of a text, which might otherwise be printed. Indeed, almost all printed books are now composed and typeset electronically, and so in theory it is as simple to output such material as an electronic file as it is to print it. This was one of the reasons for the enthusiasm that publishers initially felt about e-books: it is possible to sell the same thing twice, in different media. Not only that, but electronic copies would need no warehousing and have smaller distribution costs.

It is already difficult to remember the perhaps mindless enthusiasm for all things internet-based that prevailed in the mid-to-late 1990s, but in this climate publishers hoped that gadget mania, and the novelty of the internet, would persuade people that the best way to read a novel was electronically (Herther, 2005).

The idea that the book was doomed was taken so seriously that various printed volumes were produced lamenting its decline, such as Sven Birkerts' (1995) *Gutenberg Elegies*. Academic conferences were held on the subject of 'Beyond the Book', while scholarly volumes of essays debated the future of the book as a printed text (assumed generally to be a short one; see Chernaik et al., 1996; Finneran, 1996; Nunberg, 1996; Sutherland, 1997).

Publishers may also have been encouraged by the success of the e-journal, which had already begun to revolutionize academic library use. Readers could now access journals by searching an online database rather than using the library copy and having to photocopy if they wanted to take it home. Publishers therefore probably hoped that, in a complementary fashion, readers would be keen to visit online bookshops, download a copy of a book and read it at their leisure.

In this they were helped by software and hardware manufacturers. Several dedicated reading devices were produced by manufacturers such as Gemstar and Rocket. Software manufacturers such as Microsoft and Adobe developed proprietary formats that allowed electronic files to be customized for different reading devices, so that one particular type of book could only be read on one particular type of reader. This had significant commercial advantages, since with the use of simple digital rights management software a vendor could make sure that readers could only access a book a certain number of times before it was locked (Mooney, 2001).

In return, the customer was promised significant advantages. Books would now be more easily stored, since hundreds could be stored on one device. A round-the-world trip no longer necessitated carrying a case full of guidebooks. Instead, one e-book reader would store all the guides you could ever need. There would no longer be any problems with books being out of the library, or being sold out at the bookshop, since electronic files can be reproduced multiple times however high the demand. Books would also no longer become dog-eared, with cracked spines or stained pages. In addition, online content could be easily searched (Burk, 2001).

The fiction publisher Barnes & Noble invested especially heavily in making its list available electronically. It embarked on a high profile marketing campaign to publicize the fact that novels could now be bought and downloaded from their website.

Considering the reader

Ten years later, this e-book world seems remote, ill-considered, naïve and hopelessly optimistic. And yet it is important to consider what went wrong, and why, if we are to understand the present state of the e-book and how it may develop. It was not simply the dotcom crash and the economic chaos following 9/11 that caused the predicted e-book boom to go bust. There was also a failure on the part of publishers and software manufacturers to consider the needs and behaviours of their users and customers – whether those were libraries or readers themselves.

E-books and reading devices

It is perhaps surprising that e-books are still designed for specific types of reader and for proprietary software formats, since tying e-books to particular reading devices has always seemed ill-advised. Early e-book reading devices were relatively costly ($300–500) and in relatively short supply outside the USA; they were heavy, clunky and quite easily damaged. They proved relatively unsuccessful because customers were reluctant to spend a significant amount of money on a device that looked rather like a laptop but had none of a laptop's other functions: you could only use it to read e-books (Stevenson, 2007).

Current devices are more varied: e-books can be read on laptops, tablet PCs, PDAs or even mobile phones, and also dedicated readers like the Sony e-book reader (Fictionwise, 2007). Devices like PDAs and phones may be used for numerous functions, and thus the cost of a dedicated device is saved. However, the screens on these devices, especially mobile phones, may be small and badly lit and thus difficult to read for any length of time. New dedicated readers, like the Sony e-book reader, are designed to ameliorate this, since they are relatively small and portable but have a backlit screen intended to simulate reading by daylight. However, a dedicated device still costs $300–400.

E-books and their users

The popularity of dedicated devices like the iPod shows that there is no inherent reason why people will not buy a device designed primarily to do one thing (play music, in the case of the iPod), even though it is relatively expensive. However, the iPod delivers music in the way that we like to receive it – in other words, through earphones into our ears. The main problem faced by readers of e-books is that all delivery devices available tend to interfere with the way that we like to read – in other words by reading on paper, not on a screen. This is not only because of the problem of screen size or of lighting. Numerous studies have shown that paper has many more convenient properties than the computer screen. For example, it is easily portable, relatively light and can be folded and stored easily. It can be read almost anywhere (famous examples being in the bath and on the beach) and is easily copied and shared (Sellen & Harper, 2001). Although it is quite easily damaged it is also relatively cheap to replace. Although early e-books advertised the robustness of electronic files, which could not be torn or dog-eared, anyone who has ever dropped a PDA on a hard floor knows how fragile such devices can be, and how expensive to mend and replace.

E-book formats

One of the reasons for the success of the e-journal is that remote access to a collection makes it easier to find and access articles, which can be printed out for reading quickly and easily (Liu & Stork, 2000). They can then be stored in a folder with other articles or just disposed of after reading. This process is more convenient than having to find a large bound volume of journal issues on library stacks, and then either photocopy the article you need or read it in the library. In theory, therefore, an e-book ought to have the same element of convenience. However, a journal article is relatively short, whereas most books – particularly novels or other works of fiction – tend to be several hundred pages long. Printing out a novel would not only be expensive and time consuming (even with a laser printer), but also the resulting stack of paper would be heavy and ungainly to carry, and would probably require some sort of binding to make it easy to read and prevent pages being damaged or lost. Thus, it is probably more convenient for a reader to buy the paper copy, ready-bound, which will probably be more attractive and may be cheaper.

The continued existence of multiple software formats also causes problems for readers. If we buy a paperback novel we expect it to fit into a bag or onto a bookshelf alongside other books from different publishers. We also expect that when we have read it we can lend or give it to other readers or sell it to a second-hand book dealer. However, the analogous actions are far from easy in the world of e-books. There are still numerous software formats for e-books, which are mutually incompatible. Thus a book in the Adobe e-book format cannot be read on a device designed for Microsoft e-books. Indeed, e-book-selling websites, such as eBookMall, are compelled to produce complex tables comparing functionality for the benefit of confused prospective customers (www.ebookmall.com/aboutebooks.htm).This makes it difficult or indeed impossible for people to share, lend or resell e-books. It also means that if you have amassed a collection of books in one format, you are tied to buying specific types of software, or your collection becomes useless (Mooney, 2001). It is of course true that these restrictions apply to digital music: however, the continued prevalence of illegal downloading shows that many listeners are still unhappy about such restrictions. In the world of books readers who object need not break the law – they simply buy a paperback.

Types of e-book

So, how can we gauge the status of literary e-books? One of the easiest ways to do so is to look at what is being offered by commercial publishers and booksellers. Although Barnes & Noble was a pioneer in offering e-books, it is no longer possible to find any e-books for sale on its website. Some publishers such as Penguin offer a few titles as e-books, but the number of them (about 200) is tiny in comparison to the printed list. This may be contrasted to O'Reilly Publishing, for example, which produces titles for computer professionals and makes most of its books available electronically, either as PDFs or files to be consulted online as part of the Safari digital library. This is a collection of over 3500 titles produced by a number of publishers, including Addison-Wesley and Microsoft Publishing, on subjects related to technology and business. Oxford University Press (OUP) is also beginning to put its new scholarly monographs online at Oxford Scholarship Online, which is available to libraries by subscription. It already includes 1200 titles and is growing fast.

To explain this difference in the prevalence of different types of e-books it is again important to consider how such books are used. Academic or technical books are used much more like a journal article than a paperback novel. Users tend to searche O'Reilly computer manuals and then consult discrete chunks. The content also goes out of date very quickly, but the user need not go and buy a new edition of the book, since the online version will have been updated. Users of OUP's academic monographs are also likely to be consulting part of the book, perhaps a chapter, or skimming it for relevant information. It is relatively unusual for academic books to be read in linear fashion from beginning to end (if a reader wishes to do this it seems more likely that they will borrow the printed book from the library). Oxford Scholarship Online is therefore presented in a way that is reminiscent of OUP reference books, with reference to keyword searching, outward linking and supporting reference material. OUP also clearly envisages that parts of the books will be used to build up electronic course packs of reading for students. This is an ideal use of the online medium: it frees teaching staff from the need to photocopy different parts of several books for teaching purposes, and allows them to create a custom-made course book, taken from various sources.

Academic and technical books are therefore designed primarily to be searched and consulted, like reference books, whereas novels, biographies or popular history or science books usually have a narrative designed to be followed from beginning to end. We have seen that e-books have great advantages where material is time-sensitive, needs to be updated regularly, is required in small chunks from different sources, and is likely to be searched, skimmed or read in small parts. However, none of these factors applies to fiction and imaginative literature and so the printed book is still the vehicle for such content.

Readers also take into account financial considerations. In the case of fiction, it probably seems more cost-effective to buy numerous printed books than to pay for an e-reader and then still have to pay for the electronic content to go in it. This is a significant factor: although e-books are cheaper to produce than printed books, and carry none of the warehousing and distribution costs, they are still relatively expensive, compared to print. Some publishers have priced them artificially high, apparently fearing that the viability of their printed list may be threatened (Ardito, 2000).

Reading for pleasure

Books also have a more intangible value to readers. E-books for technologists are designed to be useful within a work setting. However, most readers of imaginative literature read for pleasure, and enjoy the book as an object. In the mid-1990s there was much discussion of the fact that the computer was a poor substitute for the beautifully bound leather volume that Birkerts laments in *The Gutenberg Elegies* (1995). Even though most people seldom see such beautiful volumes, let alone read them, the experience of choosing and reading a book is obviously a pleasant experience. Research on the UCIS (User-Centred Interactive Search) project has shown that readers take great delight in hunting down exactly the right book in a second-hand bookshop or auction catalogue (Blandford et al., 2006).

Library users have very complex ways of gathering information about books, including from the design of its cover (Makri et al., 2007). These users describe the pleasures of reading and of using libraries (although they could have equally negative reactions if the library environment was not conducive to their work; Blandford et al., 2006). However, these emotional clues and payoffs were usually absent in the digital library world. If the world of books and reading also has an emotional value, we can begin to see why those who read for pleasure have not easily been seduced away from the book to the rather unemotional experience of accessing e-content.

Hypertext fiction

Another e-book innovation which caused excitement in the mid-1990s was the development of hypertext fiction. This was a new form of fiction designed to be written and read in hypertext as opposed to linear narrative, and was therefore tied to electronic delivery. Hypertexts preceded the web, and could be created and read using offline software such as Hypercard, or the early online system Xanadu created by Ted Nelson (Nelson, 1992).

Unlike a conventional e-book, whose contents might be the same as the print version and are designed to be read in a linear fashion, hypertext fiction is designed to be read in a non-linear fashion; specific pages (lexias) can be read in a different order, depending on the path that readers decide to take from one page to the next. Writers might specify paths through the material, by providing only one link from a page, but they could also allow readers to choose different links, and as a result the story might develop in different ways depending on the lexias visited. Perhaps the most famous pioneering example of hypertext fiction was Michael Joyce's short story *Afternoon* (Joyce, 1986).

This kind of fiction has generated a great deal of interest among literary critics, led by scholars such as George Landow (1994) and Jay Bolter (1991). Its multivariate nature proved intriguing since it seemed to chime with the postmodernist and poststructuralist schools of literary theory, which insist that the meaning of texts is always variable and dependent on the reader as an interpreter. Hypertext fiction therefore seemed a way of allowing the reader to control an imaginative text. Jerome McGann even turned the activity of reading and interpreting a literary text into the multi-player Ivanhoe game, based on the novel by Walter Scott (www.patacriticism.org/ivanhoe/about/). Hypertext fiction also proved popular with writers seeking to experiment with the form of their work and ways to deliver it via the web, and has given rise to online writing communities, such as Trace at Nottingham Trent University (http://tracearchive.ntu.ac.uk/index.asp).

However, it has proved much less popular with readers. Even members of the Trace community said that they did not read e-books (Rennie, 2001). It appears that hypertext fiction has not made a transition into the publishing mainstream, perhaps damaged by the lack of success of the wider fiction e-book market. Thus it is difficult to know whether readers are unaware of hypertext fiction and would adopt it if they could, or whether the experience of potentially being lost in a hypertext world might confuse most readers, who are used to a largely linear narrative.

Beyond the e-book

It might therefore appear that the process of delivering literature to readers has been unchanged by digital technology. Although readers of literature have not flocked to the e-book, it should not be assumed that their lives have been unaffected by electronic technology. Technology has arguably had a more profound impact on the way in which we find and buy books than the way that we read them.

Although no longer stocking e-books, Amazon and other online booksellers make it possible to access millions of books by searching online. One's choice of book is no longer dictated by the buying policy of the local bookshop, and the frustration of finding numbers 1, 5 and 8 of a series of novels in the shop when you actually want number 2 is a thing of the past. We may now have almost too much choice of reading matter, but for a bibliophile this is a delightful problem to have. The functionality of the databases which run behind sites such as Amazon has been developed in an imaginative fashion to address this problem of too much choice, allowing us to see what other readers have bought, a record to be kept of our purchases and suggestions made about future reading. We can also access reviews of books written by numerous other readers. Some people may find this intrusive and annoying, but for others it helps to address the problem of not being able to consult a knowledgeable bookseller.

There are disadvantages to online booksellers, of course. In any digital collection it is, as yet, impossible for readers to browse bookshelves and find a book serendipitously. Browsing a shelf, or a small bookshop, can also give us a sense of what is available on a subject. Searching online is good if the reader already has some idea what they are looking for, but can be overwhelming. Fiction libraries, especially those for children, also concern themselves with reader development, which is impossible online. However, in contrast to e-books, it appears that the advantages that readers derive from online bookselling are enough to compensate for some disadvantages inherent to the medium.

The long tail

Another huge advantage offered by the online book retailing industry is its ability to track down what Anderson (2004) has called 'the long tail' of published books - rare and out-of-print books. These are books that are relatively seldom sold and so it is uneconomical for publishers to keep them in print. Companies such as Amazon and Abebooks aggregate and make searchable the catalogues of thousands of second-hand bookshops and private individuals. Previously, tracking down a rare volume by an obscure writer might have required a visit to numerous booksellers, or repeated phone calls or letters, yet now it is possible find the book in a single online search. Although some readers delight in rooting about in dusty second-hand bookshops, for many the convenience of online searching has been sufficient compensation.

Print on demand

Electronic publishing makes it possible to access rare content from this 'long tail' of published books in other ways. Specialist companies like Lightning Source publish them using print on demand. Readers can search for a rare title, and it will be printed for them from an electronic file when needed. This is an excellent way to combine the advantages of electronic files and print technology, allowing the reader to read the book in conventional form, and the company to store the electronic file rather than having to warehouse a large number of books.

Another form of print on demand cuts out publishers altogether. Sites such as Lulu.com specialize in what in the print world would be known as vanity publishing. This allows authors to have their work disseminated online, and even marketed through Amazon, without the agency of a conventional publisher. However, there is little sense of quality control for readers, since there is no publisher's reader to review the content. This has always been one of the most significant drawbacks of the most famous free source of e-books, Project Gutenberg. Unlike Lulu, Project Gutenberg contains digital versions of books that have already been published and are out of copyright. Thousands of books have been scanned or keyed in by volunteers. However, as a result there no way of assuring the accuracy of such texts, since they are as good or as bad as the volunteer decides to make them. This exemplifies at once the major advantage and major drawback of internet publication: readers can now find a far greater variety of material online, but the quality of much of it is extremely unreliable. This may be one of the reasons for the Google Book Search project.

Google Book Search

Google is digitizing millions of books, many of which are very rare, in partnership with several major libraries, including the Bodleian Library in Oxford and the University of Michigan Library. The books are made available for free through Google, although there are restrictions on what may be done with the text (it cannot be printed, for example). No-one is entirely sure why Google decided to do this, and some publishers and librarians are suspicious about its motivation for doing so (Pace, 2006). Crane, for example, has predicted that it will cause profound changes in the way academic libraries and digital libraries function (Crane, 2006). However, it appears that Google's motivation is to assure readers access to textual content that is as trustworthy as its search results. However, as in the case of commercial e-books, it seems most likely that Google Book Search texts will be of most use to those who want to search for material across a large corpus, rather than to read a little-known Victorian novel.

Publishers and web marketing

The internet has also affected the way in which books are marketed, and the relationship between authors and readers. All major publishers now have websites where readers can find out more information about authors and their background, and about specific books they have written. Some authors, such as Lindsay Davies (www.lindsaydavies.co.uk), have extensive personal websites on which they provide additional information about themselves and their novels, and interact with readers via online forums or e-mail. This kind of information has proven very popular with readers, who now have a new way to communicate with authors whose works they enjoy.

The successful use of the web for this kind of content has led some publishers to experiment with including such content in printed books, perhaps because they feel that readers now expect such information. Thus in the HarperCollins paperback edition of *Instances of the Number Three* by Salley Vickers (2002), we can find an interview with the author and some additional background material about the novel. This is another interesting example of how electronic publication has changed the content of some books. However, it remains a relatively rare practice, which is perhaps not surprising since it seems to be evidence of confusion about what the web and printed books do best. Books are ideal for delivering novels, and the web is best suited to additional factual content, and to being a way for readers and authors to interact.

The future of e-paper

Is it possible to make any predictions about the way the publishing market may develop in future as a result of electronic delivery? One innovation that may affect readers of literature in future is electronic paper. It was first developed by Xerox, and although it has taken a relatively long time to emerge from the developmental stage, a European company, Plastic Logic, has recently announced that it has gone into full production. E-paper is like an extremely thin, flexible computer screen. Like paper it can be rolled up and bound so that pages can turn like those in a book. Content may be downloaded onto the pages using 'e-ink' (www.plasticlogic.com/products. php). This means that books on e-paper should have the advantages of both electronic delivery and paper: readable, flexible, and portable, and at the same time easily reproduced, updated, stored and accessible via the internet (Richards, 2007).

It is too early to tell how successful e-paper may be. However, it is possible to extrapolate certain possibilities from the current usage of e-books. Although, as with all new technologies, prices are likely to fall if a large volume of sales is achieved, e-paper is likely to remain more expensive than a paperback book. As a result it seems unlikely that books of several hundred pages will be downloaded onto e-paper. Therefore it will probably be most useful for the kind of content that dominates the e-book world: technical and scholarly texts, from which readers need discrete chunks of information, such as a single chapter. Once read the text will probably be deleted and overwritten, although there may be a facility to store content on a computer hard drive, then 'reprint' it to the e-paper via a USB or wireless link when needed. The facility to download a text, read it on e-paper and then download the next document as required should mean that less printing is necessary. This will probably be especially attractive to students, and those who have to pay for printing by the page. However, it seems less likely to be attractive to readers of imaginative literature, or the kind of book (like a biography) that is usually read from front to back cover. Having repeatedly to download chapters may prove annoying, and means there is no chance to go back to re-read an earlier part of the book (often useful to readers of mystery novels, who may wish to re-acquaint themselves with earlier clues), and it also deprives us of the guilty pleasure of flicking forward to find out what happens in the end! Without usability testing it is impossible to know how easy e-paper really will be to read. However, for readers of literature, it may still be easier and cheaper to buy a paperback.

Conclusion

Electronic media are causing changes in the way that literature is delivered to readers. Online booksellers allow us to find a vast range of books, including those that are rare and out of print, with relative ease. Publishers now use the web to provide additional materials about their books and authors, and writers' websites provide an unprecedented opportunity for readers to interact with their favourite authors. However, the publication of e-books has had relatively little impact on the world of imaginative literature thus far. Paper provides a convenient medium on which to read, and is easy to manipulate and carry to various locations. It is as yet too early to tell whether e-paper will be able to rival its analogue predecessor.

Electronic delivery has not changed the publishing industry as quickly and completely as was predicted. We should probably not be surprised by this – as Vandendorpe (1999) points out, it took several hundred years for the form and usage of the printed codex book to stabilize, after the advent of printing. Although technological development has speeded up considerably, he believes that it will be at least several decades before the e-book becomes as central to our literary culture as the printed volume. It is also probable that this will happen in a way that we cannot yet predict.

In one of the most sensible of the articles written when predictions of the death of the book were rife, Dauguid (1996) argues that if a medium is useful it does not die. Instead, technologies and media supplement each other as we learn what they are best used for. Thus a manuscript is useful for writing notes or a personal letter, but a computer would be used to produce a formal document. Dauguid therefore predicted that books would not be superseded by electronic publishing, but that they would supplement each other, and this has proven to be correct. The e-book has not taken over publishing, but has found its own particular niche in technical, business and educational content. E-publication is not as well suited to the needs of readers of imaginative literature, and the book market is thriving, boosted by the use of the web as a marketing medium. Paper and electronic media complement each other, allowing readers to be both bibliophile and technophile according to their needs.

Bibliography

Anderson, C. (2004) The Long Tail, *Wired*, **12** (10),
www.wired.com/wired/archive/12.10/tail.html.
Ardito, S. (2000) Electronic Books: to 'e' or not to 'e'; that is the question,
Searcher, **8** (4), http://infotoday.com/searcher/apr00/ardito.htm.

Birkerts, S. (1995) *The Gutenberg Elegies: the fate of reading in an electronic age*, Ballantine Books.

Blandford, A., Rimmer, J. and Warwick, C. (2006) Experiences of the Library in the Digital Age. In *Proceedings of the 3rd International Conference on Cultural Convergence and Digital Technology*.

Bolter, S. J. (1991) *Writing Space: the computer, hypertext and the history of writing*, Lawrence Erlbaum.

Burk, R. (2001) E-Book Devices and the Marketplace: in search of customers, *Library Hi-Tech*, **19** (4), 325–31.

Chernaik, W., Deegan, M. and Gibson, A. (1996) *Beyond the Book: theory, culture and the politics of cyberspace*, Office for Humanities Communication.

Crane, G. (2006) What Do You Do with a Million Books?, *D-Lib Magazine*, **12** (3), www.dlib.org/dlib/march06/crane/03crane.html.

Dauguid, P. (1996) Material Matters: the past and futurology of the book. In Nunberg, G. (ed.), *The Future of the Book,* University of California Press.

Fictionwise (2007) *Reading Software and Devices FAQ*, www.fictionwise.com/help/ReadingDevicesfaq.htm.

Finneran, R. J (1996) *The Literary Text in the Digital Age*, University of Michigan Press.

Herther, N. K. (2005) The E-Book Industry Today: a bumpy road becomes an evolutionary path to market maturity, *The Electronic Library*, **23** (1), 45–53.

Joyce, M. (1986) *Afternoon, a story*, Eastgate Systems, www.eastgate.com/catalog/Afternoon.html.

Landow, G. (1994) *Hyper/Text/Theory*, Johns Hopkins University Press.

Liu, Z. and Stork, D. (2000) Is Paperless Really More? Rethinking the role of paper in the digital age', *Communications of the ACM*, **42** (11), 94–7.

Makri, S., Blandford, A., Gow, J., Rimmer, J., Warwick, C. and Buchanan, G. (2007) A Library or Just Another Information Resource? A case study of users' mental models of traditional and digital libraries, *JASIST*, **58** (3), 433–45.

Mooney, S. (2001) Digital Rights Management and the Emerging EBook Environment, *D-Lib Magazine*, **7** (1), http://webdoc.gwdg.de/edoc/aw/d-lib/dlib/january01/mooney/01mooney.html.

Nelson, T. E. (1992) Opening Hypertext: a memoir. In Tuman, M. C.(ed.), *Literacy Online: the promise (and peril) of reading and writing with computers*, University of Pittsburg Press.

Nunberg, G. (ed.) (1996) *The Future of the Book*, University of California Press.

Pace, A. (2006) Is this the Renaissance or the Dark Ages?, *American Libraries Online*, January, 2006, www.ala.org/ala/alonline/techspeaking/2006columns/techJan2006.cfm.

Rennie, I. (2001) *Bad Books: an investigation into the unpopularity of online fiction and the future of the e-book*, unpublished MA dissertation, Sheffield University.

Richards, J. (2007) Curl-Up Factor Could Spell Change in Reading Habits, *The Times*, (6 April), http://business.timesonline.co.uk/tol/business/industry_sectors/media/article1620550.ece.

Sellen, A. J. and Harper, R. (2001) *The Myth of the Paperless Office*, MIT Press.

Stevenson, I. (2007) The Book trade. In Bowman, J. H. (ed.), *British Librarianship and Information Work 2001–2005*, Ashgate.

Sutherland, K. (ed.) (1997) *Electronic Text: investigations in method and theory*, Clarendon Press.

Vandendorpe, C. (1999) *Du Papyrus à l'Hypertext: essai sur les mutations du texte et de la lecture*, La Découverte.

Vickers, S. (2002) *Instances of the Number Three*, HarperCollins.

Chapter 10

Beyond the Caxton legacy: is this the end of the book and its communities?

BOB GLASS, ANN BARLOW AND
ANDREW GLASS

Editors' preface

This chapter reviews developments in making literature available to readers and provides a number of scenarios under which the traditional book may continue to survive, regardless of the emerging technologies which are making literature available in other, competing, formats.

With their experience in library and information science education, librarianship, bookselling, reading groups and the web, the authors provide a unique perspective on developments in this area.

Introduction

While Toffler's vision of word processing leading to the advent of the 'paperless office' (Toffler, 1981) has yet to come into existence, access to literature without the use of books is rapidly gathering pace. Indeed, 600 years after the invention of the printing press, Caxton's legacy, the traditional method of making literature available to readers appears to be under threat. Over the past 15 years the world wide web has provided increasing resources, and it was inevitable that works of literature should be among those made freely available in electronic formats. In addition, more sophisticated hardware and software have enabled text to be delivered in a range of multi-media formats. In some cases, admittedly, such technologies have removed the need to read, but on the other hand they have also removed barriers to literature for many who find reading difficult or even impossible. It remains to be seen whether current experiments in the use of 'Web 2.0' technologies will further develop access to literature away from the printed word. James Bridle (2006), on his site booktwo.org, hypothesizes: 'As digital technologies become ever more prevalent, we believe it is inevitable that the primacy of the physical book will fade, and the art forms traditionally associated with it will be radically altered also.' E-books are clearly here to stay.

Historical developments

Conversion of literary texts into electronic format began as early as 1971 when Michael Hart identified the value of computers for 'the storage, retrieval, and searching of what was stored in our libraries' (Hart, 1992). This was the beginning of Project Gutenberg. The goal of Project Gutenberg was to make freely available in electronic format books whose copyright had expired (Lebert, 2004). Initially, Hart keyed in individual texts such as the American Declaration of Independence using simple code which could be easily read and searched by any system (Berglund et al., 2004). However, with the advent of the world wide web in the 1990s, Project Gutenberg could be developed into the leading repository of e-books. By the end of 1997, Project Gutenberg had released its 1000th e-text, with dozens of volunteers engaged in digitizing and proofreading (Lebert, 2005).

While Project Gutenberg maintains its goal of making works of literature freely available, the popularity of the world wide web and the commercial opportunities it offers have also led to the rise of online publishing as a means of marketing as well as distribution.

Electronic literature formats and sales

While there are a number of electronic formats for literature, the most prevalent by far is the e-book. SearchMobileComputing (2008) defines an e-book as 'an electronic version of a traditional print book that can be read using a personal computer or by using an e-book reader'. The latter includes dedicated e-book hardware, personal digital assistants (PDAs), Apple iPods and mobile telephones. Currently the most widely used distribution medium for this material is the world wide web. Techweb.com (2008) lists a range of products including Microsoft Reader, eReader, Mobipocket Reader, OPS and OpenReader.

There are clear trends showing an increase in access and sales for e-book material. Cochrane (2004), citing the Open e-Book Forum as his source, records that unit sales of e-books in the first quarter of 2004 had increased by 46% over the same period in 2003 to 421,955 units, with revenues in the same period increasing by 28% to $3,233,220. *Publishers Weekly* states that sales increased by '1,442% in January 2003 over January 2002' (Pointer, 2004). Although these are not easy to compare, as they are figures for different periods, they nevertheless show a trend. Differentiating the sales of different types of e-book in order to assess the impact on works of literature is yet more complex.

What will be the effect of format changes on traditional book communities?

Although there has been a vast increase in the delivery of e-books, this does not necessarily mean that traditional book communities are experiencing an equivalent decrease in sales. Electronic delivery may not have the predicted negative impact on the demand for printed materials. In terms of works of literature, for example, we need to ask whether these sales are additional to, or instead of, traditional book sales. There is certainly overall growth in e-book publishing, but figures from traditional outlets do not suggest that this has taken place at the expense of printed materials. E-book sales may indeed add extra sales to already healthy traditional revenues – they may make a contribution similar to that of reduced price mass-market publishing for book clubs and supermarket special editions, which are very valuable sales tools to the publishing industry. Indeed, the figures to date appear to hold the promise of increased sales for the publishing industry.

The effect on publishers

In many ways, publishers appear to be in a reasonably buoyant position in relation to book format developments. Traditional book sales figures show that sales increased by 7.7% in January–September 2007 compared to the same period in 2006, while value sales grew by 6.3% over the same time frame. Export sales increased by 12.4% in volume and 11.1% by value, while home sales grew by 4.5% by volume and by 3.4% in value' (Publishers Association, 2008). Table 10.1 reports Nielsen BookScan Monitor statistics for 1998–2002.

Table 10.1   Nielsen BookScan Monitor statistics
                  (Nielsen, 2008)

Year	1998	1999	2000	2001	2002
Total	104,634	110,155	116,415	119,001	125,390
Literature	2,930	2,936	3,150	3,130	3,270
Fiction	9,236	9,800	10,860	13,076	11,810

Even accepting the premise that sales of traditional copyright book titles may be decreasing in some areas, providing they have the digital rights publishers should be able to make this up by maximizing electronic sales. While this represents new technical and marketing challenges, there are considerable opportunities for generating new business via the web. In addition there will also be exciting promotional and co-operative opportunities available to publishers, authors and readers through the new Web 2.0 technologies. These activities might result in a greater expansion of the readership for a particular author or title than was achievable previously. A new 'interactive army' of literature consumers might well develop and increase readership levels beyond that of the previous 'print only' readership.

Although the economics of publishing are fairly complex, the origination costs for literature remain the same regardless of format up to the point of print, storage and distribution. Publishers are likely to develop appropriate models, as they always have, to support viability in the production and sale of a range of book formats. These formats include: hardback, paperback, e-book and talking book.

There is no real evidence yet that publishers will opt to publish books solely electronically – although this is not to say that promotional chapters or specific book titles might not be made available this way. Similarly, electronic publishing might allow for the trial selling of certain titles, or the publication of literature that might attract significant but rather limited consumer interest. It can be far less risky and far less expensive to make a title available electronically than to go into full production and have it fail.

It is likely also that the institutional market for literature (libraries and education establishments) will not alter their format requirements dramatically over the next few years. This will provide publishers with some stability and an opportunity to develop their e-expertise and offerings over the next decade. Increased demand for electronic textbooks, however, may be a different matter.

The pricing strategy for e-literature in comparison to traditional print is another area where policy is still developing. There is a school of thought which argues that books in e-format, as with music as MP3 files, should cost less than traditional products. This is often far from the case in reality. A number of publishers believe that, as the intellectual input is the same and that economically one format should support another, there should be little or no price differential on titles. Ultimately the marketplace will decide the outcome of this debate. Potentially, though, sales generated by reduced pricing on e-books might act as a catalyst for developing traditional sales.

The effect on bookshops

The traditional high-street bookshop has experienced difficult times for a good many years. The old sole trader model has given way increasingly to a chain-based model in many areas of the UK. Nevertheless, a strong base of independent retailers remains, surviving and developing their businesses by adapting, innovating and providing a consistent added value service to users.

The economic picture is not wholly clear. *The Bookseller* provides two contrasting reports for 2006 and 2007 on its website (www.bookseller.org.uk, 8 February 2008). UK booksellers and stationers reported a drop in sales in both December 2007 and January 2008. A CBI survey found: '[W]ith a balance of -19%, a greater proportion of booksellers and stationers experienced a drop in volume of sales between 2nd January and 16th January 2008 than an increase. For December 2007, the contrast was even starker, with a balance of -43%' (Neill, 2008). This is a worrying trend.

However, these figures contrast with the healthier picture of book sales portrayed by Nielsen BookScan (2008), which found that the consumer market grew to 33.5 m books in December 2007, a rise of 4.3% over December 2006. The four weeks to 26 January 2008 showed sales growing by 11.6% to 16 m books sold, in comparison with the same month in 2007.

A further report (Neill, 2008) states:

> Individual booksellers have also reported a positive Christmas with Borders and Waterstone's experiencing increases in like for like sales and Amazon and Play.com recording record breaking Christmases. W H Smith is expected to report positive results when its Christmas trading statement is out.

Admittedly, online sales have played a key role in these figures but, regardless, these figures do not suggest the imminent demise of printed books.

Regardless of the mixed financial messages it is clear that bookshops will need to continue to adapt and to embrace where possible e-publishing opportunities. Creating and developing a web presence in order to make e-materials available to customers would appear to be a necessity in order to ensure survival – regardless of bookshop type or size. Perhaps proactive activities, such as in-store promotion for e-book products alongside traditional book promotions, might be effective. Offering e-book downloads and subscriptions might be another way forward. It works for Amazon and others, so why not the smaller bookshop? Additionally, although the format platforms are a little unstable at present, selling e-book readers might be another useful idea. The issue of what retail models and discount structures publishers apply to e-books will also be of real importance to bookshops, and could well be critical to their ability to adapt and survive.

The effect on non-traditional book retailers

It is appropriate to consider non-traditional book retailers separately from bookshops, because their focus is very different. The traditional bookshop might sell a range of books together with posters, music products or office and art materials. They may even sell coffee and cakes! This is not the same, however, as the supermarket chains operating nationally and internationally whose books (and related materials) are really just another consumer product bar code and income stream. Supermarkets' participation and sales are very important to authors, publishers and readers alike (though booksellers might argue their right to do this) – but there is little commitment or focus on the content. If traditional book sales dry up, or new formats are introduced, they will simply adapt to the change or get out of the marketplace. Life would carry on much as before.

Shops selling books are well placed to play a key role in the expansion (or not) of e-book sales. Large retail operations can become major players in making changes to our purchasing habits, and to how and what we ultimately buy, simply as a result of their scale of operation. If there is an e-book revolution it could well begin here. If one or more of these outlets were to make available an inexpensive, effective e-book reader, provide an innovative method of repackaging e-materials and/or sell e-products at significant price differentials, this could well create considerable new demand. Whether this would reduce the sales of traditional books is unclear: customers who choose to buy an e-book may not necessarily be the same customers that buy traditional books.

The effect on public libraries

Public libraries have been adapting the services available to their users for a long time. The traditional model of making available adult/junior fiction, non-fiction and reference books has long gone as the sole purpose of a library. In addition to providing reading materials and implementing initiatives to attract and retain more readers, many libraries offer online (and offline) courses for users as well. A growing number of library authorities now incorporate 'one stop shops', providing local government information, advice and payment facilities for local services.

A key recent development in public libraries has been making web access available to all. This has involved training library staff to be IT and e-literate; these staff then pass this experience on to users.

Given the diverse nature of library services currently offered, it is interesting that many people still appear to judge the success of library services by the number of books issued. Benedicta Page's (2008) *Bookseller* article 'There's More to Libraries than Lending' begins by addressing this. She reports that library visits and book issues for 2006–7 (reported by CIPFA, the Chartered Institution of Public Finance and Accountancy), are 'not encouraging':

> The overall pattern is one of declining numbers both in general usage and specifically in book-borrowing, with a drop nationally of 1.4% in visits, down to 337.3 million, and book issues falling 2.6% overall to 314.7 million. Within that context, even the top performing libraries such as Norfolk & Norwich's Millennium Library and Birmingham's Central Library are showing dips, though small, in their numbers year on year.

She adds:

> However, the decline is not uniform: children's book issues are up for the third year, according to figures supplied by The Reading Agency. Meanwhile, visitor statistics don't tell the whole story

when much library activity now takes place outside the library building itself. And against the national decline, some councils – such as Stockton-on-Tees, Southend, Poole, Swindon and Leicester – have managed to buck the trend and increase their library usage and issue numbers.

Just like the sales figures for books and e-books, the figures for libraries are not easy to analyse and cannot just be accepted at face value.

Initiatives like 'The Big Read', 'Bookstart' and 'The Richard and Judy Book Club' are having considerable impact on the public and are clearly encouraging reading and library borrowing. Developing a literate population and encouraging citizens to read books remain key items on the government's education agenda. While reading doesn't need to be undertaken using traditional formats, it is at present. Even with the growth in e-literature it seems clear that libraries will remain a key building block in the government's strategy.

Specifically how the development of e-sales will affect libraries is difficult to predict. Book issues and user visits to libraries have been falling for a whole host of reasons. Whether the increased availability of e-books will further erode the market share of libraries is unclear. In relation to providing e-materials, specific initiatives might be appropriate. Publisher agreements with public libraries can allow library users to access e-books from library catalogues, on site or off, in the same way that universities allow their users to access e-books. Lower costs for e-materials could see a shift in the balance of formats selected by libraries, changing the balance of virtual and physical stock. There is no real reason why libraries cannot offer literature in the new formats if required.

Libraries are already offering added value and extra services in a similar way to bookshops. The ability to build on these services, to develop an enhanced online presence and to make books available in a range of formats will be major factors in whether they remain key players in the provision of literature to readers.

The effect on readers

There will always be a reader market for traditional printed fiction. Many readers feel a distinct bond with the traditional paperback and hardback formats. There is a physical, tactile and emotional interaction – it isn't the same if you're using a computer or an e-book reader, let alone an iPod or mobile phone. This isn't to say that people don't want to read fiction this way; it's just that many prefer the alternative. Could this change? Would the public choose to read the latest Harry Potter in e-format if that were the only way they could read it? The answer is clearly yes, but is this likely? Perhaps, marginally, yes. There will soon be much more choice in the formats available for mainstream fiction. E-readers are improving (although they are still rather expensive and tend to be proprietary in the way they operate), and prices for e-books may be reduced in relation to hard copy versions. What could make a big difference to the volume of literature read as e-books might be the introduction of an inexpensive, iconic iPod-type device: something attractive, very simple to use, easy to carry around and above all easy to read. No such device yet exists. The closest product is probably Amazon's Kindle e-reader.

Nevertheless, the e-book format provides for a whole host of possibilities. What if a title is out of print? What if physical publication is delayed? What if we can't get to the library or bookshop and the book can come to us? What if we want to change the typeface or text size? What if we want something now, now, now? E-books can offer a whole range of features which are unavailable in the traditional print medium. There are significant advantages to using e-books, and many users will adapt to using them for a wide range of reasons.

Conclusion: a symbiotic relationship?

Let us return to the original question. Beyond the Caxton legacy: is this the end of the book and its communities? There is very little doubt that the Caxton legacy has not yet been superseded. Traditional print is still very much used and demanded by readers and produced and distributed by publishers, booksellers and libraries. There may well be a transition, a readjustment, a development, yes, but perhaps this could best be described as a healthy, developing symbiosis allowing more people to access books and bringing more literature to readers – a relationship which would, without doubt, have met with Caxton's approval.

Bibliography

Berglund,Y., Morrison, A., Wilson, R. and Wynne, M. (2004) *An Investigation Into Free eBooks*, Arts and Humanities Data Service, www.jisc-collections.ac.uk/workinggroups/ebooks/studies_reports.aspx [accessed 15 May 2007].

Bridle, J. (2006) *About Booktwo.org*, www.booktwo.org/about/ [accessed 15 May 2007].

Cochrane, K. (2004) *The Growth of E-Book Sales*, www.epublishing-info.com/blog/2004/06/04.html [accessed 4 September 2007].

Hart, M. (1992) *Gutenberg: The History and Philosophy of Project Gutenberg*, www.gutenberg.org/wiki/Gutenberg:The_History_and_Philosophy_of_ Project_Gutenberg_by_Michael_Hart [accessed 15 May 2007].

Lebert, M. (2004) *Michael Hart: changing the world through e-books*, http://pge.rastko.net/about/marie_lebert [accessed 15 May 2007].

Lebert, M. (2005) *Project Gutenberg, from 1971 to 2005*, www.etudes-francaises.net/dossiers/gutenberg_eng.htm#1990-1996 [accessed 15 May 2007].

Neill, G. (2008) *Book Sales Down, Insists CBI*, www.thebookseller.com/news [accessed 7 February 2008].

Nielsen (2008) *Nielsen BookScan Monitor*, www.nielsenbookscan.co.uk/ [accessed 6 February 2008].

Page, B. (2008) *There's More to Libraries than Lending*, www.thebookseller.com/ [accessed 9 February 2008].

Pointer, D. (2004) *Ebook Sales Statistics 2004*, www.parapublishing.com [accessed 7 September 2007].

Publishers Association (2008) *PA Sales Monitor Statistics (PASM) January–September 2007*, www.publishers.org.uk [accessed 8 February 2008].

SearchMobileComputing (2008) *Ebook Definitions*, www.searchmobilecomputing.techtarget.com [accessed 1 September 2007].

Toffler, A. (1981) *The Third Wave*, Pan Books.

Chapter 11

Survival strategies for the independent bookseller

MIKE MIZRAHI

Editors' preface

This chapter discusses the strategies an independent academic bookseller has to adopt in order to protect and develop business in the 21st century. It provides an overview of reader base issues, the promotional opportunities available and the additional activities that are needed to ensure continued engagement with the book-buying public.

Introduction

When you walk into a bookshop and pick up a book, this is a significant achievement for the bookshop manager. In order to get to that book you may have gone to that part of the shop devoted to bestsellers or new titles. You may have gone to a particular department such as biology or philosophy. The book may have caught your attention in the shop window, or it may have been part of a particularly attractive table display visible by the front door as you came in.

All of these methods of placement can be used by the bookshop manager in order to draw attention to a new title. The market for books, however, is not restricted to those people who casually walk through the front doors of their local bookshop. So, how does a bookseller manage to promote new titles to those people who are rarely, if ever, in a bookshop?

My reality: the competition

I am the manager of a small, independent, academic bookshop in a large university town. Although there is a very large student and academic community, the reality of my situation is that I have strong competition from internet booksellers, two or three major national bookselling chains and other, smaller, operators as well. For this reason it is necessary to focus all of my attention and skills on maintaining and increasing my market share in the sector of the market in which I am operating. Like most brick-and-mortar bookshops, my business operates for customers who purchase books in my shop, and customers, who could be many miles away, who purchase books by telephone, e-mail, fax or post.

All of the methods described in this chapter have been employed over the years to bring new title information to customers in the general market, undergraduate academic market, school market and hospital library market.

The general market: which stock to select?

Promoting a new book to the market is a relatively simple procedure within the physical confines of a bookshop. The first problem we encounter in the book trade is identifying which titles to put our resources behind promoting and which to avoid.

Each month thousands of new titles become available for the bookseller to choose from. Unless a publisher has made a mistake, all of these new titles will have a market. Some of these markets will be larger than others; for example, the demand for a book on the architecture of southern Manchester can be expected to be smaller than the demand for a new Harry Potter novel.

The bookshop's buyer(s) must first look through the lists provided by the publisher, and recognize those titles that belong in the market they supply.

For an academic bookshop with a high-street presence, it is important to keep up to date with the general market, but deciding on which titles to stock and promote is a largely hit-and-miss affair.

A new work of fiction from a million-selling author would not automatically be a book I would need to stock. For example, Catherine Cookson is a hugely successful author but I have never been asked for a copy of any of her books in my shop.

Promotion: bringing titles to the attention of readers
Shop-front displays

Having identified which titles to stock, you then have to decide how to bring them to the attention of the book-buying public.

If you think demand for a new book will be high, then a sure way to let customers know that you will be selling it is to place posters in the shop window advertising its forthcoming publication. When it is published, a large quantity of copies on display in the window will alert customers to its availability and hopefully result in sales. Unless the publisher of the book is supporting it, this form of promotion can be expensive, especially if sales prove to be lower than expected.

This type of promotion would not necessarily work for all books. If the book was a work of fiction by a previously unknown author with an unattractive cover, forgettable title and little or no publicity in the media, then few sales would result and, even worse, no attention would be given by the public.

Several of the books I have promoted in this way have been books from local authors published by small publishers with little or no marketing budgets. They have not been successful due to lack of interest from the customers who use my shop; promotion of this kind does not always result in sales.

Shop windows can be especially useful, however, and you do not have to create a large display to garner sales if the title and cover of the book are right. Several years ago a book called *Women Who Love Too Much* was published. It had a plain white cover apart from its title, and did not receive a large amount of publicity. I placed a single copy in the window and before long customers were coming in to look at it many times a day. Sales were good. The book generated its own interest with the minimum of shop window promotion.

A window display can be very successful because of the large numbers of potential customers it can attract. Unfortunately, far more people walk or drive past my shop than walk in, so this is the only way many people can be notified of the publication of a new book.

Once in the shop a customer can be informed of a new title by a number of other methods.

In-shop promotions

A tabletop display can lure a customer to new titles of any genre. American fiction, martial arts and popular science are all subjects which would attract interest. Correctly signed, a tabletop display will attract most customers if only for a moment, and if the book is good enough it will then speak for itself. The bookseller can only lead the customer to a book being promoted. After that, the customer will make up his or her own mind.

Most bookshops have new titles departments. A customer entering a bookshop is often not entering with the intention of purchasing a particular title, but will often pick up a book they remember reading about a few days earlier in a review. Newspapers and magazines regularly review books that have just been published, so if you can have an area within the shop that a customer can recognize as likely to have new titles it will often be the first place they look.

Guiding the reader

Correct signage within a bookshop is of growing importance. I believe that customers are more likely to walk out of a shop without asking for the book they are looking for than ever before. There was a time when most customers who entered my bookshop would enquire at the counter if they were unable to find a particular book, but these days they are more likely just to walk straight out with no questions asked.

Posters are often available from publishers wishing to promote new titles, and can be used in a number of ways. They can be used in window displays, on tabletops, behind counters or indeed on any free space within the shop.

The academic market
Undergraduate promotions

Promoting new academic titles to undergraduates is, in my experience, a thankless task. A student at university is often only going to purchase a textbook recommended by their tutor. These lecturers have the power to make a new academic book a success. Publishers are aware of this power, and spend a large amount of time and money trying to get their new books adopted onto undergraduate reading lists. The bookshop has little in the way of marketing opportunities to promote new textbooks successfully.

Occasionally, we do have a closer relationship with a lecturer than the publisher. When a lecturer makes themselves known by regular visits to the bookshop, this relationship can result in the possibility of promoting new titles from many different publishers. Unfortunately, only a few of the largest publishers have sufficient resources to promote books directly to university lecturers, and this results in many new titles not getting the promotion they may deserve. However, the job of the bookseller is to stock books they feel will sell. So if a new textbook comes out on a subject they know is studied at the local university, but the current recommended title is written by the tutor, it is highly unlikely that the tutor will decide to recommend the new book. It would be the job of the university library to stock the new book, but not the bookshop.

Promoting books to academics

Of course it is not only university undergraduates that one hopes to sell to, but also postgraduates and senior lecturers. Most academic publishers have over the years attempted to build large databases of lecturers' names linked to their subject areas. When they bring out what they hope will be a successful new title on a specific subject, they use these databases to send free copies out to lecturers teaching that subject in the hope that the book will be adopted as suggested reading for students the following year. Unfortunately, these databases quickly become out of date as lecturers retire or move to different universities, and without constant updating publishers often find their computerized information incorrect. We still receive information from publishers sent to the bookshop's old address. This changed 15 years ago and, despite numerous attempts to get corrected, this still carries on. If publishers would take the simple step of consulting the local university bookshop they would be able to target their (our) customers much more accurately.

The school market

Schools order books for a number of different reasons. They have libraries they might wish to improve, classrooms that require teaching materials and, finally, teachers who might want to keep up to date with the latest teaching developments.

We have discovered over the years that the role of the a bookseller in promoting new titles to schools has gradually diminished, as other ways of accessing this information have increased. School librarians no longer have to visit a bookshop in order to view recently published titles. They can request information online from publishers and access any number of reputable websites giving out recommendations. Because of the pressures on their time, they have increasingly adopted these methods at the expense of diminishing their contact with the local bookshop. This is not true in all cases, as there are still librarians who acknowledge and value the role of the local bookshop, but as this shift continues it becomes increasingly difficult to give the same excellent service to fewer and fewer libraries. Book recommendation has always been a two-way process. Not only did the bookshop pass on information about new titles and popular requests to the librarian, but the bookshop received information back about the librarian's customers' requests, which in turn could be used to inform other librarians.

As a school supplier, most of our business is in supplying new textbooks written either to improve on existing textbooks or to meet the needs of a changing curriculum. The market is very large and dominated by a few publishers who are very keen to get their books adopted by schools – to the extent of giving very strong inducements in the way of large discounts. Indeed, the discounts offered to schools to purchase books direct from the publisher are often greater than those that can be offered by the bookshop to stock them. In their increased desperation to get this business, publishers have decided in many cases to try to exclude the local bookshop. The bookshop has therefore little or no reason to try to promote new textbook titles to schools; the publisher by and large does this.

The medical library sector

Over the years this bookshop has supplied many books to the NHS. Long before the internet and direct competition from publishers, most of the information gathered by hospital libraries and hospital staff regarding new titles came from book reviews in medical and nursing journals and the local medical bookshop. If there were no medical bookshops local to the hospital, it was very difficult for the hospital librarian to make accurate judgements on new book information. It was because of this that this bookshop expanded into medical book supplies several years ago. We took in new titles from many different publishers and arranged book displays within hospital libraries that could be attended by doctors, nurses and other health professionals as well as the hospital librarian. These visits were very well appreciated, and good sales would result. Close ties were built up between the libraries and bookshop, with the result that the bookshop staff would understand which particular subject areas were important to each library. With this information each library could be supplied with relevant new title lists throughout the year, garnered from information obtained from publishers. Information would be passed on regarding new books from the large publishers, and also from small and medium-sized publishers. The system worked well and discounts would be given that libraries could not obtain from publishers at the time.

Unfortunately, a few years ago the NHS decided that it would prefer take control of who supplied hospital libraries at a national level. If a library had a budget greater than a given amount it would be directed to get its supplies from one supplier; this supplier would be awarded the contract after tender. Whether this resulted in savings I am not in a position to judge, but I do know that many libraries were forced into going to suppliers they got little or no service from. This happened several years ago, and to this day I am told about the dissatisfaction among many people about the system.

As a result it was not possible for us to continue to arrange these displays for the larger libraries, as any book sales resultant would be to a competitor.

Conclusion

Selling newly published books in this day and age is increasingly difficult for many booksellers. Many of the media outlets responsible for helping to promote new books are also trying to make money by selling them (newspapers, journals and television).

Publishers who historically would help bookshops promote new titles are often now trying to sell their new titles direct to the consumer in direct competition with the bookshop.

Despite all this competition, many people still purchase books from a brick-and-mortar bookshop. Identifying and promoting new titles to these customers is still an important part of the job of the bookshop manager. Using specialist knowledge that is often not available to publishers, a bookshop can often increase the expected sales of a new title with skilful promotion.

Chapter 12

All this and chocolate too: educating new professionals in reader development

SUSAN HORNBY

Editors' preface

This chapter discusses the role of the academic and practitioner in ensuring that issues and developments within the field are articulated for future professionals. It outlines the creation and implementation of a specific 'Literature and its Readers' unit for undergraduate and postgraduate students. It then examines the unit's contents and the reaction of both practitioners and students to the unit.

Introduction

During the academic year 2000–2001 the undergraduate programme offered by the Department of Information and Communication at Manchester Metropolitan University was reviewed. During this process, a colleague (Margaret Kendall) and I re-evaluated our teaching and came to the realization that our joint experience and interests could be used to structure a unit that would enable our students to follow the link from author to reader and discuss the issues involved in reader development.

Margaret and I worked together to design a unit which would meet both the academic requirements of the university and the professional standards required by CILIP accreditation – and would, we hoped, prove enjoyable, provocative and challenging for our students. This chapter will examine the unit in detail and report on the responses from students, external examiners and practitioners.

Background

Web page design, knowledge management, information auditing, information and communication technologies, search engines, information systems design, financial management, human resources management, legislation, political and governmental information, information access, information retrieval, censorship, surveillance, privacy, confidentiality, information for education, health, business, information literacy . . . and on and on.

The above are just some of the areas of professional expertise our undergraduate and postgraduate students have to address during their time at university. It is breathtaking in its range and scope, and sometimes seems like a helter-skelter of essential knowledge, understanding and skills. Somewhere there also has to be space for students to take time to pause and reflect on the benefits and joys of works of imagination to individuals. This was something we aimed to address with our new unit.

Student intake

The unit was designed as an elective. This meant that, depending upon timetable constraints, students on all programmes offered by the department could enrol on the unit. We decided to design it as a level 3/postgraduate unit, which meant that postgraduate students could take the unit with undergraduate students (with appropriately modified assessments and learning outcomes).

The students' backgrounds were varied, from full-time undergraduates straight from school or college with limited professional practice to part-time mature postgraduate students with wide experience of information work. In addition to the differences in their professional knowledge and academic qualifications, the students came from a variety of social backgrounds. We have mature students with family commitments, students from overseas and students whose first language is not English. The varied professional and personal experience of the students could have been seen as a disadvantage, but in fact we have found that it enhanced the delivery of the unit.

As the unit was an elective (that is, not compulsory to any programme of study), the uptake has differed from year to year. In one year 35 students enrolled, and in another only 12.

Syllabus

'Literature and its Readers' (the title of the unit) is about the pleasures and benefits people of all ages gain from reading imaginative literature. It covers all aspects of the chain which links author to reader. It includes how relevant organizations work together to support and promote reading for all tastes. Recent developments, including the growth of reading groups and the use of the internet, are highlighted.

In detail, the syllabus includes:

- the historical development of children's literature
- stages in reading development and books for various age groups
- multimedia publishing
- literacy initiatives including Bookstart and other early-reading initiatives, and literacy initiatives in education
- storytelling
- electronic resources, such as websites for children and their reading
- the range of literary and popular fiction for adults
- cultural diversity
- authorship and readership of different genres of popular fiction
- marketing literature
- the reading industry, including writers, illustrators, publishers, booksellers, libraries, literature officers and the arts funding system
- current issues, developments and partnerships
- the roles of public libraries in reader development, including advising readers and organizing events, activities, reading groups, and the uses of ICT (e.g. reader-related sites on the web, software assisting readers with selection)
- managing literature in libraries: sources of information for selection, acquisition policies, promotion and stock arrangement, user surveys, monitoring and evaluation, and strategies for providing socially inclusive services
- regional specialist collections.

This became the weekly programme outlined in Table 12.1.

Table 12.1   Weekly programme

Autumn term

Week	Lecture
1	Introduction to the unit Historical development of children's literature
2	Child development and reading development What makes a classic children's book?
3	Recommended reading for pre-school, infant and primary school-age children Prizes for children's literature
4	Storytelling for pre-school, infant and primary school-age children
5	Sharing stories: your recommended reads
6	Recommended reading for teenagers Promoting reading to teenagers and young adults
7	Introduction to the topic for debate Promoting reading to children: national initiatives and the use of ICT (online)
8	Current issues and trends in reader development work with children and young people
9	Poetry and its readers
10	Tackling social exclusion through literature
11	End of term debate

Spring term

12	From author to reader The book trade Publishing and marketing books
13	Conservation and preservation Special collections
14	Fiction for adults and public libraries: past and present
15	Hypertext: transformations
16	Managing fiction in libraries: sources of information
17	Partnerships: the key to successful reader development
18	Get Into Reading
19	The roles of imaginative literature in people's lives Reading groups
20	Managing fiction in libraries: genre fiction
21	Reader development work with visually impaired people

Unit outcomes

We wanted students to explore the full range of imaginative literature, the needs of readers of all ages, the organizations providing access and support and the issues currently affecting the industry.

After completing the unit, students were aware of the range of imaginative literature for children and adults, had an understanding of the reading development of children, had an understanding of the constituencies involved in the reading industry and the relationships between them, had an understanding of the role of public libraries in reader development and promotion of the arts and literature for adults, and were able to identify strategies for the effective management of imaginative literature in libraries.

Teaching methods

We used a variety of teaching methods, including lectures, group discussions, student-directed learning, talks from visiting speakers and laboratory practicals. We tried to vary the presentation and utilize the experiences of our students.

Practitioners

One thing we were clear about from the very beginning was that we would make the most of the knowledge of practitioners. We as academics could outline the historical and theoretical aspects of the topic and examine and discuss proposed developments, but we felt that those who had everyday experience of the issues would be an invaluable source and an inspiration to the students. In this we were correct; the most frequent comments from students when evaluating the unit were 'Great guest lectures' or 'Guest lecturers were inspirational'. Many of the contributors to this text have presented sessions to our students.

WebCT Vista

As the time we had was limited early on, we decided to make use of WebCT Vista, an online support system for learning and teaching. Margaret Kendall was the initiator of using WebCT Vista but I now use it for all my units and find it invaluable. In 'Literature and its Readers' we used it for discussion groups, 'the great debate' and specific online tutorials.

It is an excellent way of communicating with students. We have found that students enjoy it and appreciate the flexibility it provides. Margaret has written an excellent article on the first use of the software (Kendall, 2002).

The great debate

It was clear early on that the unit had been chosen by lively students who enjoyed reading and enjoyed talking about the things they read. The lead-up to the Christmas vacation is always a difficult time, in terms of keeping students enthusiastic about the learning, as so many other activities compete for their attention. After some discussion we hit upon an idea that has proved popular, educational and fun: the great debate.

Five weeks prior to the end of term we introduce a topic for debate. We divide the students into two groups: for the motion and against the motion. Using WebCT we set up two closed online discussion groups, so that only the students in the relevant group can see the relevant discussion. The students use the discussion groups to outline their arguments for debate. On the final day of term the students meet together in their groups for 45 minutes and discuss their strategy. We then have a formal debate.

Topics have included:

1   Great book or great video? The Big Read top 100 books contained many books recently made into feature films or television serials. The Big Read top 100 reflects the recent viewing rather than reading of the public.
2   This house believes that children should be encouraged to read a canon of classic titles rather than indulging in formulaic fiction or the latest popular craze.
3   This house believes that 'teenage fiction' is a genre created by desperate publishing houses to sell more books, particularly to frantic parents and target-chasing libraries.

As you can imagine, the debates were 'lively' but fortunately no blood was spilled. Students really engaged with the topics and used the discussion groups to outline and prepare their strategies. We had very few 'no shows' on the final day of teaching before the Christmas break, despite the fact that the unit was timetabled in the 4.00–6.00 session – never a popular time.

Storytelling

Part of the syllabus covers storytelling. Again using WebCT, we set up a storytelling discussion group and encouraged students to post stories they had enjoyed as children or enjoyed sharing with children. We then presented a lecture on storytelling and shared a story with the group. The students knew that they would have to share a story suitable for a specific age group the following week.

This session usually takes place around Halloween and there have been funny stories, scary stories, sad stories and happy stories. It is interesting just how much students and tutors enjoy this session. At the end of it students are asked to post, on WebCT Vista, a bibliographic reference to the story they shared; this builds up to a cohort-specific recommended reading list for children. Many students who have graduated have told me that they find this list useful in their first professional post.

This session has been useful in other than academic terms, in that it has given me ideas for Christmas presents and has introduced me to authors and stories I had never read before.

Assessment

The unit was assessed via two pieces of coursework: one relating to children's literature and reading development, the other relating to the promotion and management of literature for adults in libraries.

We decided that as these were final-year students at least one of the assessments for both postgraduates and undergraduates would be a work-related presentation. As the size of the group differed, and students had experience of assessed presentation on other units, we decided that they should prepare overhead slides with accompanying notes and handouts for 50% of the mark and write a focused report for the other 50% - without actually having to give the presentation.

Students commented that they found this useful in terms of preparng for job interviews and appreciated not having to stand up in class and present.

Feedback

We collect feedback from students, external examiners and contributors, both formally via unit evaluations and reports and informally in conversation.

We have found that students loved the discussion groups, using them to communicate with staff and other students. The benefit of using an online system is that (with luck) it is available 24/7 and students can post at any time. On one memorable occasion one student posted a message for the great debate at 2.30 a.m. on the day of the debate.

As mentioned previously the guest lecturers have proved inspirational and popular. Students have had mixed feelings before the storytelling session, often feeling anxious at first, but both formal and informal feedback has been positive for this session. Students have commented that it was one of their favourite sessions and that the atmosphere was 'supportive'.

Feedback from practitioners and external examiners has also been positive.

There is a section on the unit evaluation form which asks if there is anything that could be improved in the unit. Memorably, one postgraduate student wrote: 'Nothing - it's too much fun.'

Conclusion: and chocolate too

Well, you have read this far and no mention yet of chocolate. How then does chocolate relate to this topic?

Linda Corrigan, who has been a guest lecturer since the beginning of the unit, now jointly presents it with me. Her original sessions were about making literature available to people with visual impairments, and to illustrate this she used chocolate.

She would bring two boxes of a well known chocolate. One she would leave as the manufacturer intended, but she individually wrapped each chocolate from the other box in brown paper. Students chose from the first box using sight, taking much time to choose their favourite. Then they were asked to choose from the second. They were then asked to choose another with eyes closed, and to open it and eat it if they wanted. Some ate, and some didn't. Reasons why they didn't were varied from nut allergies to really disliking the coffee-flavoured chocolate and not being sure what they were holding.

The problems they encountered choosing their favourite the second and third time illustrated how difficult it could be for a visually impaired person to select a book without access to its jacket and the blurb, and the problems of someone else choosing for you.

So there you have it. Literature and its readers - and chocolate.

Bibliography

Kendall, M. (2002) Adding An Extra Dimension: the experience of using WebCT for the Literature and its Readers unit, *Learning and Teaching in Action,* **1** (2), www.ltu.mmu.ac.uk/ltia/issue2/kendall.shtml.

Section 5

Afterword: the reader as author

Introduction:
Section 5

Finding a book group, let alone the right book club for you, can be a tricky task. In this chapter Francine Sagar recounts her experience of taking part in book groups. In a very amusing but incisive way she discusses not only the literary but also the psychological goings on, in what for many is just a very nice social event. Isn't it?

Chapter 13

A bookworm's eye view: choosing the right book group for you

FRANCINE SAGAR

Editors' preface

The reader is the ultimate consumer: without readers what would be the point of publishing books? Book groups can stimulate, educate and entertain the individuals who belong to them. What can be done to ensure that they will continue to exist and thrive, and what can library and information professionals learn from the groups?

Introduction

I am a teacher, a mother, a wife and an ordinary member of the public. As an individual who has experienced some of the many facets of what it is like to belong to a book group, I'd like to share with you an overview of the main aspects of the experience. As well as describing the actual book group processes, I will also discuss some of the more personal details which are particular to me in the context of the events I relate.

Background

There is no denying that the number of book groups has been increasing in recent years. It could be argued that these groups are formed by people who seek a new form of self-improvement at a time when evening classes have seen numbers dwindle dramatically. A book group usually meets informally about once a month, and therefore offers more flexibility than a series of weekly classes, where an examination often looms at the end of term. We should not underestimate the significance of the fact that membership of a book group requires far less commitment than more formal classes or meetings, not least since there is virtually no cost involved, as opposed to hefty night-school fees, and also because each session is independent from the others. Whereas you may not dare show your face again if you have missed two or three lessons of 'Spanish for Beginners', you know that you will be welcome again at the book group. This, in turn, makes the bond more informal due to the absence of the risk of failure: you can walk out of a book group without feeling that you are in any way deficient or inadequate, as you might have done if you dropped out of a structured class. Moreover, there is no qualification prerequisite – other than the ability to read – and neither is there any membership signing-in procedure.

I attribute my personal desire to discuss books to my long-standing enjoyment of learning. Having completed a part-time degree in English literature, I found myself missing the weekly contact with other students – two-hour slots in which texts would be examined, compared and contrasted, ideas exchanged and theories explored under the guidance of a skilled tutor.

Nevertheless, the reading matter may not be the whole story. Very early on in the life of my present (second) book group, an article was circulated in which it was argued that reading gatherings tend to offer far more than just a literary experience. The writer suggested that regular meetings of minds would often lead to the emergence of a support network and even the birth of strong friendships. I have heard similar comments from female friends who belong to book groups up and down the country, and in my native France.

I began to consider the extent to which the books themselves were central to the functioning of a book group, as opposed to the bonding between members. Does the choice of books matter, or the way they are chosen? In what ways do the members' backgrounds (sex, age, education, socio-economic circumstances, etc.) influence the outcome? Is the book group just an excuse for a get-together? And what about the recom-mendations of those such as the 'Richard and Judy Book Group' or the long-standing programme *Bookclub* run monthly by Radio 4 for the benefit of its listeners, who for the most part never get to meet other than virtually and 'on air'?

Finding a book group

How does one actually come to join a book group? I knew for a long time that a book group met at my local public library on every first Tuesday of the month – or was it every first Thursday? Perhaps it's significant that I could never make myself care enough to remember which day. Only once did I make the effort to walk the 300 yards from my house to one of the meetings. On that occasion there was a speaker talking away. Was it the rows of chairs facing the front which I did not find conducive? Or was I not made to feel welcome? I am not usually shy about joining in discussions, even with strangers. The title of the next book meant nothing to me and I felt no strong desire to read it. That, for me, clinched it and I never went to the group again.

It seems that, in my case, there was a strong element of comfort at the thought of being 'chosen', of being invited to join – as opposed to turning up and offering my two-penny-worth. I was asked whether I would like to take part in a new group on the verge of being formed, and I jumped at the opportunity.

My first book group: a useful journey

This first book group comprised a friend of mine along with a number of her colleagues and work acquaintances. They were all female and ranged in age roughly from mid-30s to mid-50s, all professionals and all middle class – which also describes me. However, I found that my background and aspirations were somewhat different from theirs, and I rejoiced at the new opportunities and challenges that would no doubt arise. From the start, and after a brief discussion, there was an assumption that this would be a 'girlie' group and that no men would be invited to join; I soon came to suspect that this was due to the desire for regular, if gentle, male-bashing that my co-readers seemed to rejoice in – not that I didn't join in, by the way!

What worked for me

The format was decided upon by consensus; I, for one, did not have any strong pre-conceived opinions one way or the other regarding such matters as frequency or length of meetings. It was agreed that we would read a book roughly every six weeks, and then meet at one another's houses in turn for a bit of supper and a discussion, always on a Friday night. This set-up was partly dictated by the fact that members lived across a wide geographical area, so it would often be impractical to go home after work then meet later.

The convivial aspect of meeting over a meal as well as a book started us up in a good light, and the occasions were very pleasant indeed, usually with the addition of a glass of wine for the non-drivers.

What didn't work for me

However, this plus-point became a strong minus for me. Quite simply, the commitment required for a whole Friday evening out was not sufficiently outweighed by the enjoyment I derived from the occasion. I often found that the time spent discussing the book was far shorter than that spent socializing, leaving me somewhat frustrated.

I wondered whether, more than the company, the choice of books itself played a large part in my increasing frustration. I felt that the titles, which were always chosen by individual members in turn, did not often elicit much interest in the others. Consequently, some of the ladies would simply not bother to read the book, while we were sometimes made to read material that we would never otherwise choose. Therein lies a paradox, since this is exactly what a good book group can do: open your horizons and give you the opportunity to expand the range of genres you encounter in your reading life.

During the short conversations on the topic of the book, I frequently formed the impression that we were defending or attacking the book, rather than discussing it. This was probably compounded by the decision we had made at the first meeting that we would score each work, and keep records of these scores. To this day, I cannot fathom how, after about a year, we reached the situation where at each meeting we would go through a complicated scoring system – scoring five criteria such as style and characterization – only to store away these incomprehensible lists of marks in the anticipation of someone eventually producing some sort of chart showing how we had rated the different books.

Book titles

Titles ranged from a number of contemporary, American female-written novels such as *Dinner at the Homesick Restaurant*[1] to a classic in the form of Henry James's *The Turn of the Screw*.[2] The latter proved to be the most elevating experience for me, possibly because of the rich nature of the text. Not only did I gain vast enjoyment from the reading itself, notwithstanding the challenge it presented for me since its structure is complex and the material disturbing, but the discussion afforded us much more in-depth analysis than any of the other books before or since.

First group review

I cannot deny that my belonging to this book group led to a widening of my reading scope, and I must stress that this has, in itself, been a very valuable experience indeed. For instance, I had the opportunity to read Jonathan Coe's *What a Carve-Up!* [3] – very much a novel of its time which I had not had the opportunity to read when it was published in the 1980s, but which I appreciated all the more with the insight of an added 20 years or so. I would further state that having to read books that I did not like, and would never in a month of Sundays have actively selected, was also good for me in a perverse sort of way, inasmuch as it afforded me the prospect of discrimination for the future. From having to plough through *My Sister's Keeper* by Jodie Picould,[4] I now know for certain that my dislike of what I rightly or wrongly class as 'chicklit' is not just visceral or vaguely based on a pre-conceived prejudice, but very much the result of having tested the genre and found it sorely lacking in respect of what I personally expect – and crave – from a good book. Furthermore, the experience has strongly reinforced my deep-seated feeling that my reading time is a precious commodity, which I am not prepared to waste lightly. Whereas before I may have struggled to finish a novel simply because a friend had recommended it to me, and I would not have the confidence necessary to reject it for fear of hurting his or her feelings, I now find that I can be firmly assertive and 'cut my losses' by giving up on a book if it does not deliver absolute enjoyment, or at least interest.

So there I was, about a year into a book group which I was finding increasingly at odds with my aspirations, and making noises about leaving after the next book, or possibly the book after next, so as not to offend anyone – when out of the blue the opportunity arose to join a brand new book group.

My second book group: coming home

Julia had simply placed a small ad on the community noticeboard outside the village post office, inviting interested parties to e-mail or telephone her. Was she taking a risk? Would hundreds of unsuitable applicants start pestering her? Would anyone contact her at all, given that so little information had been provided, apart from a desire to set up a book group? Or would dozens of would-be members contact her, and logistical nightmares ensue? Assuming that she must be experienced in setting up this sort of organization, I e-mailed Julia with just a few sentences outlining my background. Within a few weeks she organized an initial meeting at her house, where just seven women met for the first time.

I am still puzzled as to the likelihood of such a random assembly achieving any sort of unity, but, amazingly, we did. It turned out that Julia was a young professional who, having become pregnant, was now facing non-working life in a village where she had lived for a number of years without ever meeting anyone. The others ranged in age from 30-something to over retirement, some with toddlers and others with grown-up children, some working and others not. The only common factors seemed to be residency in the village (with the exception of one of my friends from the nearby town, who had asked me to bring her along) and a desire to read and discuss books. I was very sceptical about whether we could possibly become a homogeneous entity, let alone agree on book choices or a *modus operandi*.

I still don't have the faintest idea how it all happened, but happen it did. Our hostess greeted us with drinks and nibbles, whereupon the workings of our group were rapidly established, following informal suggestions by various members and then gentle discussion reaching consensus. For example: 'Shall we read about a book a month?' and 'Perhaps we could meet on different days of the week so that nobody is inconvenienced by other regular commitments?' We agreed to limit our membership to about seven or eight purely because if we were going to meet at each other's houses any larger group would be difficult to accommodate. We also discussed very briefly the notion that we would prefer to be an all-women group, establishing that this suited us all without going into much detail as to the reasons why, other than jokingly alluding to the fact that men 'would try to boss us around'. I believe we really were nervous that male members would indeed be domineering. One member has subsequently reported that her husband keeps making suggestions like 'I think your group should read this book' - which she finds preposterous!

The group gets started
At that first meeting some people had brought newspaper cuttings with book

reviews, and we somehow agreed to read *Tokyo Cancelled* by Rana Dasgupta.[5] One of the ladies offered to approach a local bookshop for possible discounts on the purchase of multiple paperback copies: names, addresses, telephone numbers and e-mail addresses were collected by the simple expedient of a scrap of paper being passed around. A date, time and venue were arranged for the next meeting and we all filed out after less than two hours, buzzing and full of anticipation.

This is the point where it could all have gone horribly wrong, particularly for me since with my usual bravado I had offered to coordinate the next meeting – that is to say, our very first discussion – and to host it. I soon realized that the choice of book had been a little unfortunate to say the least: *Tokyo Cancelled* was definitely not the 'modern *Canterbury Tales*' that the blurb had led me to believe – not a collection of simple stories. Instead, I was confronted with a complex text, or more accurately a series of texts, which got my gung-ho attitude to literary analysis flat on its back. In the end, I welcomed my fellow readers with a good deal of apprehension and a sheet of suggested topics to kick-start the discussion; this culminated with what I regarded as the all-important question: 'Would you recommend this book, and if yes, to whom?' This has become our benchmark at subsequent meetings.

Unbelievably, we had a very satisfying discussion, each member finding something to contribute and everybody listening to the others' arguments. Although we had all found the book difficult, we also agreed that reading it and, more importantly, discussing it with the group, had been a worthwhile exercise – which we wanted to repeat with other books! Our next choice was not going to be so challenging but no less stimulating: *The Five People You Meet in Heaven* by Mitch Albom.[6]

The metamorphosis

The meetings have carried on at the rate of one a month. For some of our members with very busy lives, this is all the reading for pleasure they get. As well as pure fiction, we have also read a couple of historical novels: *The Naming of Eliza Quinn*[7] and *March*.[8] We have explored African literature with *Purple Hibiscus*[9] and *Things Fall Apart*,[10] and even read some children's literature relating to the holocaust.[11] For our Christmas meeting we chose a book of poetry by a local author, and were delighted when she came to read some of her work to us and talk about the writing process while sharing our nibbles and damson gin!

In an effort to denote assimilation, I have coined the nickname 'BooKlub', a term which has readily been accepted by all. Tired of seeing paperbacks in supermarkets marked with such recommendations as 'Shortlisted by Richard and Judy's Book Club', I have printed a set of stickers that say 'BooKlub Choice' and which we affix to our own copies of the books we really like. I believe that this gesture is symbolic of our desire to stand on our own feet and be ourselves, even if we are only an obscure little group.

A kind of natural homogeneity had developed and the BooKlub is slowly evolving into a friendship network. Every book we have read has led our collection of individuals towards developing into a group entity, through sharing not just ideas but also personal perceptions and experiences. For instance, *We Need to Talk About Kevin*[12] was absolutely seminal in opening up an understanding of various aspects of motherhood, when we candidly conversed about our individual experiences; this particular text, and the notions we uncovered during our discussion of it, have often informed part of subsequent conversations on other texts.

From a personal point of view, I must add that my family has also been affected by my belonging to a book group: my husband has read and enjoyed some of the titles, in particular *We Need to Talk About Kevin* and when my son came home from university, I asked him to read it too, since I wanted to hear his point of view on both the novel and the issues raised. Over the past few months I have been diagnosed with cancer and received treatment, and a 'spin-off' has been my reading another of Mitch Albom's books *Tuesdays with Morrie*,[13] which I discussed separately with some of the members who visited me during my convalescence and soul-searching episode.

During a recent telephone conversation I mentioned the book group to a male acquaintance and he was very interested to find out how I had come to join such a circle; he expressed an interest in belonging to one too. Since he lives in the Lake District I suggested that he could either make enquiries about any existing local book groups or indeed start one himself. However, he confessed that although he liked the notion he would probably never get round to doing anything about it. I have come across a number of female friends who belong to a book group similar to mine, but I do not know of any men-only book groups, although I am sure there must be some. One of my friends and her husband had joined a book group where all the members were couples, but since splitting up, although they have remained on excellent terms, neither she nor her ex-husband have attended the group's discussions. It may be that the very informality which endears people to each other around literary pursuits prevents them from being completely detached once their circumstances change.

I now regard the other members of the group as my friends, and indeed I sometimes meet up with some of them for coffee quite separately from any BooKlub business. Conversely, I also still read avidly the titles we agree upon and I always look forward with great anticipation to the next discussion. Our meetings now tend to last a little bit longer than was originally the case, chiefly because we still devote a couple of hours to the book prior to 'indulging' in some social chit-chat. Drinks and nibbles are offered, but food has remained auxiliary to the main business in hand.

The once and future group

We are still going strong, with a membership of around eight, since two new friends have been brought along and fitted in really well with the original six. Sadly, our founding member, Julia, is emigrating, and we are also losing my friend from town, who is going to work abroad for a couple of years. Our group has stuck to the original format, and I have taken over the mechanics of e-mailing everybody with dates, titles, etc. Clare still bulk-buys the books for a small discount from our local independent bookseller, and the titles are still decided upon by general consensus.

We have examined mostly contemporary novels, but we are soon to read Keith Waterhouse's *Billy Liar*[14] and some of us went to see the film adaptation. This will lead us to read the play also, and discuss aspects of transferring from the page to the stage (or screen). Recently we have read another play, *Skirmishes*,[15] which regretfully is no longer staged, and we were joined by the playwright herself, who now writes for television, to discuss writing texts other than novels, as well as aspects of stage adaptation. The evening was a resounding success and everyone found it immensely stimulating.

Conclusion

From my point of view, as a member of the general public, a book group can be a very good thing indeed. While the road to success might not always be smooth, I really do recommend that you try to join one – or more, for that matter. Although there may be some frustrations and decision-making required along the way, it is well worth the effort. I wish you every success in finding a group that brings you as much joy and reward as my group brings to me.

Bibliography

1   Tyler, Anne (1992) *Dinner at the Homesick Restaurant*, Vintage.

2   James, Henry (1994) *The Turn of the Screw*, Penguin Books.

3   Coe, Jonathan (1995) *What a Carve-Up!*, Penguin Books.

4   Picould, Jodie (2005) *My Sister's Keeper*, Hodder and Stoughton.

5   Dasgupta, Rana (2006) *Tokyo Cancelled*, Harper Perennial.

6   Albom, Mitch (2005) *The Five People You Meet in Heaven*, Time Warner Books.

7   Birch, Carol (2006) *The Naming of Eliza Quinn*, Virago Press.

8   Brooks, Geraldine (2006) *March*, Harper Perennials.

9   Adichie, Chimamanda Ngozi (2005) *Purple Hibiscus*, Harper Perennial.

10 Achebe, Chinua (2006) *Things Fall Apart*, Penguin Books.

11 Boyne, John (2007) *The Boy in the Striped Pyjamas: definitions edition 2007*, Random House Publications.

12 Shriver, Lionel (2006) *We Need to Talk About Kevin*, Serpents Tail.

13 Albom, Mitch (1997) *Tuesdays with Morrie*, Doubleday.

14 Waterhouse, Keith (1998) *Billy Liar*, Thomas Nelson.

15 Hayes, Catherine (1983) *Skirmishes*, Dramatists Play Service Inc.

Index